The 23rd (Service) Battalion Royal Fusiliers (First Sportsman's)

Colonel, The Viscount Maitland

The 23rd (Service) Battalion Royal Fusiliers (First Sportsman's)

during the First World War
1914–1918

Fred W. Ward

LEONAUR

The 23rd (Service) Battalion
Royal Fusiliers
(First Sportsman's)
during the First World War
1914-1918

by Fred W. Ward

First published under the title
The 23rd (Service) Battalion
Royal Fusiliers
(First Sportsman's)

Leonaur is an imprint
of Oakpast Ltd

ISBN: 978-0-85706-124-9(hardcover)
ISBN: 978-0-85706-123-2 (softcover)

http://www.leonaur.com

Publisher's Notes

In the interests of authenticity, the spellings, grammar and place names
used have been retained from the original editions.

The opinions of the authors represent a view of events in which he
was a participant related from his own perspective,
as such the text is relevant as an historical document.

The views expressed in this book are not necessarily
those of the publisher.

Contents

Forewords

The Sportsmen
Sportsmen of every kind,
God! we have paid the score
Who left green English fields behind
For the sweat and stink of war!
New to the soldier's trade,
Into the scrum we came,
But we didn't care much what game we played
So long as we played the game.

We learned in a hell-fire school
Ere many a month was gone,
But we knew beforehand the golden rule,
"Stick it, and carry on!"
And we were a cheery crew,
Wherever you find the rest,
Who did what an Englishman can do,
And did it as well as the best.

Aye, and the game was good,
A game for a man to play,
Though there's many that lie in Delville Wood
Waiting the Judgment Day.
But living and dead are made
One till the final call,
When we meet once more on the Last Parade,
Soldiers and Sportsmen all!

Touchstone (of the *Daily Mail*).

The history of any New Army battalion is a valuable contribution to the history of the war. This applies particularly to a battalion like the 23rd Royal Fusiliers, which achieved a high morale and maintained excellent discipline throughout the war.

At the Front our only knowledge of the New Army before they came overseas was gained from the Brigade Staffs and Commanding Officers of the new Formations, who were sent over for short attachment to troops in the line.

We learnt from them the great difficulties that had to be overcome in raising new units, with very few officers, warrant officers, and N.C.O.'s to lead the new force and instruct them in military routine. Without exception they were filled with admiration of the physique, intelligence, and spirit of the men who had rushed to arms in those dark early days of the war.

It was evidently the flower of the nation that came forward, and probably in the history of all wars such magnificent material has never been equalled.

My acquaintance with the 23rd Battalion Royal Fusiliers extended from the end of 1916 to March, 1919, when the Battalion left the 2nd Division, and it is interesting to look back at my first impression of the Battalion, as I had not previously had any New Army battalions under my command. Regular battalions have the pride of history to sustain them, and traditions to live up to, but here I found a battalion not two years old, with its history in the making, but with the same spirit and self-consciousness that one finds in the old formations.

Those who have not had considerable experience of troops in peace and war may imagine that regiments are, at all times, sustained by a great pride in their past, and a determination to live up to it. Alas! in some cases this spirit dies away in adversity. I have seen the 23rd Royal Fusiliers in good times and in bad, and I have never found them downhearted.

When out for a few weeks' rest and training, in pleasant surroundings, their work and play were carried out with much life and zest.

In the fighting in the Cambrai salient, in the Bourlon-Moeuvres Ridge, on November 30, 1917, when the 2nd Division defeated six successive attacks on their line, the 23rd Royal Fusiliers at the end of the day held their line intact. This action was followed two days later by a withdrawal which was necessary to get us out of a sharp salient. This entailed very hard work and constant trench fighting, extending over several days. The troops were very exhausted from the extremely heavy calls that had been made on them, but after a few days' rest it was almost incredible how rapidly they had thrown off their fatigue and how good their spirits were.

They knew they had killed large numbers of Germans, and had successfully defeated a German attack which, if successful, would have been a great disaster for the British.

A more trying time was the March retreat in 1918. Lieutenant-Colonel Winter had lost his voice from the effect of several days of very heavy gas shelling of the Highland Ridge just before the Germans launched their attack, and he was voiceless for the next ten days. A large proportion of his Battalion were similarly affected, but time after time during the retreat they turned and fought, and inflicted heavy losses on the enemy until they did their share in repelling a heavy attack at Beaumont Hamel, where the Germans were finally held.

It was the spirit of such battalions as the 23rd Royal Fusiliers that broke the German offensive, and the marvellous power of recuperation that they had, given a few days to rest and sleep.

In the offensive operations that lasted from August 21, 1918, to the Armistice, the Battalion delivered many successful attacks with undiminished dash and courage, and it was a proud day when I saw them march through the Square in Duren with fixed bayonets, headed by the few Regimental pipers that had been through the war with them since their formation.

Well had they earned their Victory March into Germany, and Lieutenant-Colonel Winter was justified in his great pride in their fine appearance and magnificent transport.

In conclusion I must pay a tribute to the private soldiers, the non-commissioned officers, and the young officers, who, year in and year out, faced death and the greatest of hardships with that dogged courage that has always broken the hearts of our enemies. The saying that the British soldier never knows when he is beaten has never been truer than in this war.

My hope is that histories such as this may have a wide circulation, so that mothers, wives, and children may know what their men have done for their country, what dangers they have faced, and what vast sacrifices they cheerfully made.

From Major-General R.O. Kellett, C.B., C.M.G.

The story of the 23rd Battalion Royal Fusiliers cannot fail to be a fine one. Every soldier who, like myself, had the honour of fighting, I may say, shoulder to shoulder with it, will read its history with the deepest interest.

As its first Brigadier, I took up that appointment on December 19, 1914, when the Battalion was in its infancy, deficient of arms and equipment, but full of men whose physique, zeal, and spirit were magnificent, and this spirit was fully maintained, to the honour and fame of the Battalion, in the face of the enemy in France during the winter of 1915-16, and throughout 1916 and 1917, during which time it was in my (99th) Brigade, which formed part of the 2nd Division.

Throughout the heavy fighting we went through during this period, the 23rd Battalion Royal Fusiliers never failed me. What they were ordered to do they did, and more; any objective they seized they held on to, and never retired from. Few units can boast of as proud a record as this.

Many hundreds of their best and bravest made the last sacrifice, but the splendid gallantry and dogged and cheerful endurance of the Battalion never lessened.

I was, and am, a proud man to have had such a Battalion in my Brigade, a Battalion second to none amongst those who fought for the Empire in the Great War.

Formation of the Battalion, the Honours Gained, and Its Record in Brief

RAISED IN LONDON IN 1914 BY MRS E. CUNLIFFE-OWEN
(NOW MRS. STAMFORD, O.B.E.)

PARTICULARS OF STRENGTH.

	Officers.	Other Ranks.	Total.
Total strength of Battalion on embarkation	31	1,006	1,037
Total number of reinforcements who were posted to and joined the Battalion whilst overseas	188	3,762	3,950
Total number who have served on the effective strength of the 23rd Royal Fusiliers whilst overseas	219	4,768	4,987

Note.—The above figures do not include those posted to the Battalion for record purposes only, and who never joined the Battalion in the Field. The figures represent only those who have served on the effective strength of the Battalion overseas.

COLONELS IN COMMAND.

Colonel Viscount Maitland. From formation of Battalion to January 29, 1916.

Lieut.-Colonel H.A. Vernon, D.S.O. From January 31, 1916, to May 23, 1917.

Lieut.-Colonel E.A. Winter, D.S.O., M.C. From May 24, 1917, to April 14, 1919.

Lieut.-Colonel F.L. Ashburner, M.V.O., D.S.O. From April 15, 1919, to March, 1920.

The Battalion proceeded overseas on November 15, 1915.

CASUALTIES SUSTAINED.

	Officers.	Other Ranks.	All Ranks.
Killed in action	26	427	453
Died of wounds	2	128	130
Wounded in action	81	2,216	2,297
Missing in action	19	331	350
Died from sickness whilst on active service	Nil	11	11
Total	128	3,113	3,241

HONOURS AWARDED

D.S.O.	5
Bar to D.S.O.	1
M.C.	27
Bar to M.C.	5
Order de l'Caronne	1
D.C.M.	14
M.M.	93
Bar to M.M.	6
M.S.M.	8
French *Croix de Guerre*	1
Belgian *Croix de Guerre*	1
Italian Bronze Medal for Military Valour	1

MOVEMENTS OF THE BATTALION AND BATTLES
IN WHICH IT TOOK PART.

1915

November: Bethune sector.
December: Cambrin sector.

1916

January: Festubert sector.
February: Givenchy sector.
March: Souchez sector.
April: Souchez sector.
May: Souchez sector.
June: Carency sector.
July: Somme and Battle of Delville Wood.
August: Somme, in support.

September: Hebuterne sector.

October: Redan.

November: Battle of Beaumont Hamel.

December: Battalion resting.

1917

January: Courcelette sector.

February: Battle of Miraumont.

March: Battles of Greyvillers and Lady's Leg Ravine.

April: Vimy Ridge and battle in front of Oppy.

May: Battle for and capture of Oppy-Fresnoy line.

June: Cambrin sector.

September: Givenchy.

October: Battalion resting.

November: Battalion moved to Herzeele, behind Passchendale, ready to go in, and was then moved south to meet the German counter-attack at Bourlon Wood.

December: Holding Hindenburg line.

1918

January: Highland Ridge.

February: Highland Ridge.

March: German attack. Battalion fought a rearguard action from Highland Ridge to Mailly-Mailly.

April: Battalion holding line at Blairville and Adnifer.

May: Battalion holding line at Blairville and Adnifer.

June: Holding line at Adnifer and Ayette.

July: Holding line at Adnifer and Ayette.

August: Battalion led off for the Third Army on 21st inst., attacking and capturing enemy positions near Courcelles.

September: Battalion attacked and captured part of the Hindenburg line at Doignes, and later helped to capture Noyelles, and attacked Mount sur l'Œuvres.

October: Battalion attacked and captured Forenville.

November: Battalion attacked and captured Ruesnes.

November and December: Battalion marched forward into Germany.

1919

Battalion in Cologne area as part of Army of Occupation.

Battalion in Cologne area until it was disbanded in March.

A New Type of Soldier

With the formation of the Sportsman's Battalion it will be admitted quite a new type of man was brought into the British Army. Public Schools battalions, the Chums, the Footballers, and other battalions were formed. But to the First Sportsman's belongs the honour of introducing an actually new type.

To begin with, it was cosmopolitan. Practically every grade of life was represented, from the peer to the peasant; class distinctions were swept away, every man turned to and pulled his bit. To illustrate what is meant one hut of thirty men at Hornchurch may be mentioned.

In this hut the first bed was occupied by the brother of a peer. The second was occupied by the man who formerly drove his motorcar. Both had enlisted at the same time at the Hotel Cecil, had passed the doctor at the same time at St. Paul's Churchyard, and had drawn their service money when they signed their papers. Other beds in this hut were occupied by a mechanical engineer, an old Blundell School boy, planters, a mine overseer from Scotland, a man in possession of a flying pilot's certificate secured in France, a photographer, a poultry farmer, an old sea dog who had rounded Cape Horn on no fewer than nine occasions, a man who had hunted seals, "with more patches on his trousers than he could count," as he described it himself, a bank clerk, and so on.

It must not be thought that this hut was an exceptional one. Every hut was practically the same, and every hut was jealous of its reputation. Scrubbing day was on Saturdays as a rule, and it was then that the "un-char-lady" side of various men came out. They were handling brooms, scrubbing-brushes, and squeegees for the first time in their lives, but they stuck it, and, with practice making perfect, it was surprising to what a pitch of cleanliness things eventually got.

Even church parade has been dodged on a Sunday morning in

order that three pals might unite in an effort to get the stoves blacked, the knives and forks polished, and a sheen put on the tea-pails.

One may smile about these things now when in civilian life again, but it was all very real at the time. The First Sportsman's were not coddled; no man thought twice about getting in a terrible mess when domestic duties had to be performed. The only kick came when the hut windows had to be cleaned with old newspapers. The man who had forgotten to wash the old cloths or buy new ones came in for a terrible time.

Rivalry, perfectly friendly in character, was great in the earlier days before chums began to be split up as the result of taking commissions. If we were digging trenches "somewhere in Essex," our particular sector had to be completed quicker and be more finished in character than any other. Jobs were done at the double if it were thought to be necessary; if any man developed a tendency to take a rest at too frequent intervals—well, he was ticked off in the most approved fashion. It all made for the good of the whole. The N.C.O. in charge had an easy time, he hadn't to drive a man. All he had to do was to see that in over-eagerness his working party did not take risks.

But the time came when the calculations upon securing a commission began to make their appearance. It may be some men were approached on the matter, or that others thought they would get to the Front more quickly as individual officers than as members of the Battalion (as indeed proved the case in many instances), but certain it is that the Colonel began to be inundated with applications to apply for permission.

Whilst freely recommending all suitable applications, the Colonel, in order to keep up the strength of the Battalion, made a rule that an applicant was to supply two other recruits to the Battalion of a certain height and of absolute physical fitness.

Naturally this was conformed with, and the recruiting sergeants round Whitehall were all the richer for it. So, too, were the recruits, and everyone was satisfied. If one man went two others took his place.

Finally, as it was found that men constantly leaving was interfering with the internal organization of the companies, a special company was formed of all those waiting for their commission papers to come through.

This company, "E," proved the friendly butt of all the others, one wag even going so far as to christen it the "Essex Beagles," alleging they did not "parade," but "met"!

First Inspection of Battalion: Hyde Park, October, 1914.

So, in order to free the others for harder training this company provided very nearly all the fatigue parties for the camp.

Still, this didn't matter. It just gave the budding officers a chance to show what they were capable of. On several occasions a member of "E" Company proved he was more than a little useful with his hands when it came to a matter of treating things from a physical point of view and cutting the cheap wit out. The fatigues were also done without a murmur, that was another point of honour, and although the available strength of the company was dwindling day by day, "grousing" about extra work was conspicuous by its absence.

There was a funny side about this dwindling of the strength, too. Men would be on the morning parade, and not on that later in the day. The explanation was a simple one. Their papers had come through. A man would walk out through the gates and be pulled up by the sentry.

"What about your pass?" the latter would ask.

"Got my discharge," would be the reply.

"Got a commission?"

"Yes."

"Good luck, old chap. I'm getting my papers tomorrow."

So, many of the original members of the First Sportsman's Battalion were scattered about on every front in their various regiments. Walking through the Rue Colmar, Suez, one day I met my old company officer, then in the Royal Flying Corps. At Sidi Bishr, on the banks of the Mediterranean, I met another. A fellow-sergeant in the Battalion came up in the Rue Rosetta, Alexandria, and claimed me.

Out beyond the Bitter Lakes, east of the Suez Canal, I met an old Sportsman who had been a fellow-corporal with me. Back of the Somme, a prominent West Country Sportsman shouted a greeting to me from the Artillery. He still remembered rousing the camp at Hornchurch one night by sounding a hunting horn.

In an Artillery Captain in the Hebuterne sector I recognized another member—a Machine-Gun officer rolled up smilingly on the way up the line, and, finest time of all, I had nearly a whole day with what was left of the old crowd when they were resting after Delville Wood.

Friendships made in the First Sportsman's Battalion were not easily broken. We are out of it now, but—once a Sportsman, always a Sportsman. That, at least, has been my experience.

And it must not be forgotten that to Mrs. Cunliffe-Owen is due the credit of conceiving the idea of a battalion formed of men over the then enlistment age, who, by reason of their life as sportsmen, were fit and hard. Approaching the War Office, she obtained permission to raise a special battalion of men up to the age of forty-five. This was how the Sportsman's Battalion was actually brought into being.

Training at Home

Formed almost as soon as the war broke out in 1914, the First Sportsman's Battalion may have provoked some criticism. It was uncertain at first as to what branch of the service it was to represent. Personally I thought it was to be mounted, and I was not alone in this idea either. More than a few of us got busy at once in settling how, if possible, we could provide our own mounts. That was in the days when we were new to war, long before we began to know what something approaching the real thing was.

Recruiting went on briskly at the Hotel Cecil, London, where Mrs. Cunliffe-Owen and her staff worked hard and late. Lieutenant-Colonel Winter, then Second-Lieutenant Winter, with his ledger-like book and his green-baize-covered table, was a familiar figure. So, too, was the tailor who had been entrusted with the task of fitting us out with our uniforms. He, poor man, was soon in trouble. The stock sizes could be secured, but stock sizes were at a discount with the majority of the men who first joined up. They wanted outside sizes, and very considerable outside sizes, too, for the average height was a little over six feet, and the chest measurements in proportion.

Still, we recognized that these things had to be, and we kept on with a smile and a joke for everything. Perhaps we had a pair of army trousers and a sports-coat. Perhaps we had a pair of puttees, and the rest of the costume was our own. It didn't matter. It was good enough to parade in off the Embankment Gardens. It was good enough to route march in through the London streets. And the traffic was always stopped for us when we came home up the Strand, and proceeded down the steps by the side of "the Coal Hole" to the "dismiss." Rude things might be said to us by the crowd, but there was a warm spot in their hearts for us. We just carried on.

Bit by bit we were provided with our uniforms, and we began to fancy ourselves as the real thing. We began to make new friends, and we were drawn closer to those we knew. We came from all over the world. At the call men had come home from the Far East and the Far West. A man who had gone up the Yukon with Frank Slavin, the boxer; another who had been sealing round Alaska; trappers from the Canadians woods; railway engineers from the Argentine; planters from Ceylon; big-game hunters from Central Africa; others from China, Japan, the Malay States, India, Egypt—these were just a few of the Battalion who were ready and eager to shoulder a rifle, and do their bit as just common or garden Tommies. The thought of taking a commission did not enter our minds at the start. Every man was eager to get on with the work, with but a dim thought of what it was going to be like, but worrying not a bit about the future.

In a few weeks the Battalion had learnt how to form fours, to wheel, and to maintain a uniformity of step. Every man was desperately keen; to be late for parade was a great big sin. And this despite the fact that every man had to come into London from all parts of the suburbs, and farther out than that in many instances, by train (paying his own fare) every morning.

So the time went on. Then came the news that we were to go into camp at the Grey Towers, Hornchurch, Essex, and next came the formation of a fatigue party to go on ahead and get things ready for the reception of the Battalion. There was a rush to get into this party as soon as the news went round. Everyone was eager to do something fresh, and, after all, we didn't know what fatigues were in those days. So the party went on ahead.

We who were left kept on with our drills; we even did physical jerks on the slopes of Savoy Street, Strand. Then came the news that we were to march away. That bucked everybody up tremendously, for, to tell the truth, we were really beginning to get tired of the London life. Some of us, who had seen life in various parts of the world previously, were sighing again for the open air. All of us were thinking it was really time we did something to justify our existence. We did not claim to be show soldiers; we wanted to get at it.

Marching away from Hyde Park to entrain for Hornchurch.

All things come to those who wait, however. We were to move to Hornchurch—the first step to active service. We had our uniforms, we even had white gloves, and at last we fell in, by the Hotel Cecil, with a band at our head, and off we went. Funnily enough, some of us felt this break with London more than we felt anything afterwards. It was really our first introduction to "the Great Unknown."

Had the Guards been marching away they could not have had a greater and a more enthusiastic send-off. The streets of the city were packed; it was a struggle to get through. At Liverpool Street we were reduced to a two-deep formation, and even then it became a case of shouldering your way through those who had gathered to wish us "God speed." But we were entrained at last; we detrained at Romford, and we marched to Hornchurch. We were in the camp.

Our First Surprise.—That's when we had the first surprise sprung upon us, for we learnt that the camp would be our home for a whole solid fourteen days. No one was to be allowed to go into the village; we were to begin our course of instruction in discipline. There were a few heart-burnings, but nothing more. The Battalion played up to its ideal.

We were drilled early and late; we were instructed in the art of guard mounting; we peeled potatoes in the cookhouse; we fetched coal from the quartermaster's stores; we fell in to get our rations from the cookhouse; and last, but not least, we began to grouse. That was our first advance to becoming real soldiers. At least, so the author was told by an old N.C.O. who had marched with Roberts to Kabul, and who was again in the Service, too aged to do more than to instruct, but not too aged to do that well.

Hard work and plain but plentiful food soon made the Battalion as hard as nails, a phrase coined by the London *Evening News*, and a phrase that stuck. Quite as important, too, was the fact that a member of the "hard as nails" Battalion had to prove he was capable of acting up to it. So it was just a matter of honour that every man should keep off the sick parades, and not come home in the ambulance when a long route march or a field day was indulged in.

This took a bit of doing sometimes, for there was no mercy shown us. We said we wanted the real thing, and, between ourselves, we got it. A march of seven miles to the scene of operations, a hard field day, and a march of seven miles home again, with pack, rifle, and full equipment in other ways, was our lot. We began to recognize that we were really soldiers, and we patted ourselves on the back.

Sport, too, played a very big part in our training. The Army of to-day recognizes the fact that athletics makes and keeps our youngsters fit and well. Our Colonel recognized it from the start, and as we had plenty of material to work upon we went right away with it. We had a "soccer" team, a "rugger" team, and a cricket eleven. The records of the matches we won, and the fact that very few defeats were notched up against us, proves we had a perfect right to style ourselves "the First Sportsman's Battalion, the 23rd (Service) Battalion Royal Fusiliers."

Scullers, footballers, boxers, runners, wrestlers, actors, musicians, artists—all these could be had for the asking, and we drew upon them liberally. We were given plenty of opportunities to indulge in our passion for sport in the ordinary way, but the private who once asked for leave in order to go grouse shooting didn't get it. It was suggested he might put in a little time at the rifle range instead. No restrictions, however, were put upon any early morning running matches, and the football and cricket teams were helped in every way.

To get back to the purely military side, however. We groused at the amount of drills and night operations, to being hut orderlies, going on guard, and so on. But we did them as a means to an end. Then we had the rudest shock of all. We learnt we were to embark on the task of digging trenches—somewhere in Essex! That put the lid on things, so we considered. We, infantry soldiers, to dig trenches! It couldn't be right. We thought the Engineers, or the Pioneers, or somebody else, always did that. Our job was to carry a rifle, and to shoot Germans. That's how the rank and file looked at it in the first place. Of course they discovered other things when the Battalion got to France, but that's another story.

However, it had to be done and, like everything else, it *was* done. After an early breakfast, the company detailed fell in and marched off to the station. After a while, a special train arrived and we scrambled in. In the interim, it may be mentioned, packed trains proceeding cityward went by, the passengers cheering us. That passed the time if it did nothing else.

Nearly an hour in the train, a march of perhaps a couple of miles, and we reached our objective. Mysterious personages, with a big "G.R." in gold on scarlet armlets popped up from somewhere, produced plans, and informed our Company Officer that trenches had to be dug at such and such a place. As a rule it was somewhere where the water from an adjacent brook would percolate through the earth and make things uncomfortable. That's by the way, though, and after

THE CAMP: HORNCHURCH.

INTERIOR OF A HUT: HORNCHURCH

all it was good practice, this working out a method of trench drainage on our own. As a matter of fact we had a lot of Civil and Colonial Engineers in our ranks, and so we put all the mistakes made by the others right. Whenever possible, of course. One or two things, it must be admitted, beat us.

Sometimes it rained, sometimes it snowed, occasionally, very occasionally, it happened to be fine. But we got on with our work, waiting for the bugler to blow for the midday lunch. When "cookhouse" went we straightened our backs, got *some* of the mud off our boots, and proceeded to take what the gods (in this case the quartermaster) were good enough to give us. We always had two guesses, and we were always right. It was either bread and cheese, or bread and bully. If we were fortunate we might be able to purchase beer at a local hostelry, or Oxo at a village shop. If not so fortunate, the waterbottle or, if again lucky, a pocket-flask was brought into service.

The Kindly Shopkeeper.—Digressing for a moment, though, it may be mentioned that the various shopkeepers were always very, very good to us! They always supplied us with what we needed, if they had it, and they never put the prices up to us! At least, not much. For instance, if a resident could buy a pair of bootlaces for a penny, we were only occasionally charged more than threepence. Other things were in proportion, and Essex today has quite a lot of nice new shops, unknown before the advent of the First Sportsman's Battalion. It is pleasing to remember that a Navvy Battalion followed us!

To resume the trench digging. As we were later complimented on the quality of the work we did, we must have shone in the way of handling the pick and the spade. At the end of our labours, when the "fall in" was sounded, we were quite ready to say we were looking forward to a hot meal in our huts in camp, where, outside, the breezes whispered through the branches of the trees lining the drive, where the moon silvered the tin roofs of our living quarters, and all was bright and jolly—in the sergeants' mess!

So time sped away, and still we kept on wondering if we were forgotten. We sat by the fires in "stoves, hot, combustion slow," and we told the tale of the two highly placed War Office officials who were discussing the war years after it had finished. One had asked the other how the Sportsman's Battalion had shaped in "the Great Adventure," and then would come the climax. "Good God!" the other would say, "I've forgotten them. They're still at Hornchurch!"

All things have to come to a finish though, and so we found. We had night attacks, some three and four day route marches, even a recruiting march through Barking and its neighbourhood, we did our shooting tests, got through our bayonet exercises, had battalion drill in the early mornings, with a fair amount of ceremonial drill thrown in as a makeweight, and then came the rumour that a real big move was to be made, such a move that the departure for the Front could not be long delayed.

This was the move to Clipstone Camp for brigade training. We had heard so many rumours previously that we did not believe this, the latest, at first. But it was correct, and at last the Battalion, formed up in hollow square, was found on the parade ground at Grey Towers, where the Rector of Hornchurch bade us God speed and good cheer.

A few days later the Battalion, leaving two companies behind as depot companies, entrained at Hornchurch for the new camp at Clipstone.

There it went through brigade training, was equipped with its regimental transport, and afterwards moved to Candahar Barracks, Tidworth, to undergo divisional training with the 33rd Division, of which it formed a part.

Finally, after being reviewed with the Division by Queen Mary, acting in place of His Majesty the King, who was suffering from his accident sustained in France, all was in readiness for the next and biggest move of all.

Service Overseas

The day of the move overseas arrived. This was on November 15, 1915, when the regimental transport entrained at Tidworth for Havre, followed one day later by the Battalion, which proceeded to Folkestone, Boulogne being reached on November 17, Ostrohove Rest Camp being the first objective. No time, however, was wasted there, for on November 18 the Battalion entrained at Pont-de-Briques, joining the transport which had come up from Havre.

It was at Steenbecque, reached a day later, and where billets were found in barns and farmhouses, that the sound of artillery in action was first heard by the Battalion. Four days were occupied here in sorting things out generally, the companies parading, route marching, and being inspected.

On November 23 a move was made to Busnes, the first part of the route being over badly cut up second-class roads, and the remainder on *pavé*. The men, the war diary tells us, marching in greatcoats, and carrying blankets, found the march very trying. Billets in the area La Miquellerie were reached at 3 p.m. Distance, 11½ miles.

Then came a very important thing from a soldier's point of view. Pay was drawn from the Field Cashier, and distributed for the first time in France. Next came the notification that in conformation with the policy of re-forming the 33rd and the 2nd Divisions by forming brigades, each consisting of two new battalions and two regular battalions, the 99th Brigade was to lose the 17th and 24th Battalions Royal Fusiliers, receive the 1st Royal Berks and the 1st King's Royal Rifle Corps and join the 2nd Division.

On November 25 the Battalion paraded to march to their new billets at Bethune, being inspected *en route* by General Walker and the Staff of the 2nd Division. General Walker's opinion was that the 23rd Royal Fusiliers was one of the best battalions he had seen in

Bethune.

Still moving, on November 26 the Battalion marched to Anne-quin, Fosse 9, and owing to the road being frequently shelled, orders were given that seventy-pace intervals should be kept between platoons east of Beuvry. To improve matters, it may be mentioned, there was a heavy fall of snow, and in the portion of the village south of La Basse the majority of the houses were in ruins, the result of frequent bombardments by the enemy.

Then began the first experience of the Battalion in warfare. Before being trusted to hold a line by itself it had to serve an apprenticeship. This was done by attaching, in the first place, platoons, then companies, and then the half-battalion to battalions in the line in order to learn the work and what was expected of them.

During this time much kindness was experienced from the regular battalions to which the attachments were made. The units of the Battalion not doing attachment duty were used for working parties in the trenches and suffered several casualties. No. 2 platoon, right flank company, specially suffered, being caught by shrapnel fire on the Bethune-La Basse road, ten N.C.O.'s and men being wounded.

On December 10 instruction in the use of the gas helmet was given. Every man was required to pass through a hut sprayed with chlorine gas ten times as strong as would be used on ordinary occasions, General Kellett being present while this was being carried out, and himself going through the test.

So things went on until December 19. On that date the Battalion marched to Cambrin support point to relieve the 1st Royal Berks and take over a sector "on its own." In the trenches, No. 1 Company was on the right, adjoining the 1st King's Royal Rifle Corps, No. 2 Company on the left, adjoining the Argyll and Sutherland Highlanders, No. 3 Company was in the centre, and No. 4 Company was in support at Annequin (Fosse).

It was a very busy time, for No. 3 Company held command of the sap head at New Crater, a spot where German snipers were particularly troublesome. A gas attack was ordered upon the enemy, but, much to the disappointment of the officers and men, it proved a "wash-out" owing to the breeze dying down at the last moment. On December 21, however, as the wind was favourable, a gas attack took place on a front of about a mile. It was on this day that Captain Cameron, of No. 1 Company, was wounded in the arm by a piece of high-explosive while entering the front line.

Then the Battalion, less No. 4 Company, was relieved by the 1st Royal Berks, and proceeded to reserve billets at Annequin (Fosse) on December 22. Not for complete rest, though, as it is generally understood by the civilian, for working parties had to be detailed; indeed, on December 24 all four companies were out, less sick and those on duty. And, says the war diary, no straw was provided for the billets, no coke, coal, or wood for the drying-room, and no facilities for drying or cleaning clothes.

Christmas Day in the Trenches—On Christmas Day the Battalion paraded for trench duty to relieve the 1st Royal Berks, the trenches taken over being the same as were occupied on December 19-22, with the alteration in disposition that made No. 4 Company replace No. 3 Company in the centre.

There was also a special bombardment on this day, and the Battalion's first patrol, consisting of four men and an officer, went over the parapet, being out in No Man's Land for an hour. During that time the party located a sniper's post, cut out some wire from the enemy's entanglements, and were persistently sniped at themselves, while great difficulty was experienced in maintaining direction.

Then, on Boxing Day, Colonel Lord Maitland was wounded in the knee by a piece of high-explosive while proceeding to the 99th Brigade Headquarters *via* Cambrin Church.

The German snipers continued their activity, there were intermittent bombardments, several casualties were sustained, and on December 29 the Battalion was relieved by the 18th Royal Fusiliers. Owing to the bad state of the trenches this relief did not take place until 5.10 p.m., although it was due to be effected at 3 p.m.

Still, the Battalion got back to its billets at Annequin (Fosse), and on December 30 marched back to Busnettes for sixteen days' divisional rest. Owing to the very arduous work which had been done since December 19, on this occasion no packs were carried, and only three men fell out in a tiring march of 11¼ miles.

1916

The New Year opened quietly, the usual rest-time routine of kit inspection, squad drill, route marching, and so on, being indulged in, a draft coming up from the base on January 7, while on January 11 the first leave for officers commenced. Then came a move, and on January 19 the Battalion marched to Le Touret, relieving the 6th Queen's Regiment, the 99th Infantry Brigade taking over a sector of the front at Festubert from the 37th Infantry Brigade.

On January 22 the Battalion relieved the 1st Royal Berks, "B" Company being in reserve in the old British line, "A" Company in support in Richmond Trench, "C" Company in front line Cover Trench and Islands, and "D" Company in front line Orchard Trench. The front line and support line garrisons, it may be noted, had to take up their positions over the top, and so could not be visited in daylight. The position remained the same until the then *Kaiser's* birthday, on January 27, when although the order for relief was given at 6 p.m., a "stand to" was ordered in anticipation of an attack.

This did not come off, and, the relief by the 24th Royal Fusiliers being effected, the Battalion marched back to Bethune on January 28, where the billets were inspected by General Kellett.

On January 29 Colonel Lord Maitland relinquished the command of the Battalion, temporary command being taken by Major Richey, D.S.O., and Lieutenant-Colonel H.A.Vernon (1st King's Royal Rifle Corps) assumed command on January 31, while Lieutenant Cooper was appointed machine-gun officer in place of Lieutenant Lewis, who had been wounded.

Le Quesnoy was the next move, made on February 3, and relieving the 1st Royal Berks on February 7, the Battalion was in turn moved out of the trenches into the village line Givenchy on the 11th, remaining there until the 15th, when it again relieved the 1st Royal Berks in B3 sub-sector Givenchy. On the 17th the Battalion was relieved by the 16th Royal Welsh Fusiliers and moved to Le Quesnoy, remaining there until the 27th, when it proceeded to Barlin. On February 28 another move was made to Petit Sains, relieving the 22nd Royal Fusiliers, and on the 29th the Battalion took over the Souchez North sector of trenches from the French 77th Infantry Regiment.

From March 1 to March 13 the Battalion held the line at Souchez North in turn with the 1st King's Royal Rifle Corps and on the latter date proceeded to billets at Noulette, returning again to the trenches on the 17th, the Battalion on the left being the 17th Royal Fusiliers, and on the right the 1st Royal Berks. Then on March 28 it moved to La Comte for divisional rest.

Reclinghem was the next move, made on April 9, and on April 11 there was a Brigade field day, another reinforcing draft arriving on the same day. Then on the night of April 21-22 the Battalion relieved the 1st King's Royal Rifle Corps in the Souchez second sector of the line. So the end of the month arrived with alternate duty in the trenches

Lt.-Col. H.A. Vernon, D.S.O.

and rest in billets.

More reinforcements, to replace wastage, arrived in the early part of May, and on the 23rd the Battalion was in the trenches at Berthouval, marching to its billets at Camblain l'Abbé on May 30. Working parties were naturally provided for the trenches while the Battalion was resting, and two men were accidentally wounded on the 4th. But things were moderately quiet until the night of June 10-11. On that date the Battalion relieved the 17th Middlesex Regiment in the Carency left sector of the front.

On June 21 Lieutenant-Colonel Vernon was wounded whilst visiting a sap head held by Jerry Delaney, the boxer, Major H.V. Pirie assuming command of the Battalion until he returned to duty. The Battalion was relieved by the 1st King's Royal Rifle Corps on the night of June 22-23, and proceeded to billets at Villiers aux Bois. The next move, on the 27th, was made to Estrée Cauchie.

The Somme Fighting.—Then came the move to the Somme and the July of 1916, when the average life of the infantry subaltern in France was only worth three weeks. Many, indeed, were killed within a week of their crossing the Channel, on the very first day of entering the trenches and taking part in the British advance. The 23rd Royal Fusiliers were engaged in the whole of the desperate fighting on the Somme, including the battle of Delville Wood, the story of which is told in another part of this volume.

Following this bath of blood, on August 1 the Battalion left Bund support trench, two companies going to Longueval Alley, and two remaining to garrison and dig trenches at Montauban.

Becoming united again, on the 29th the Battalion, under the impression that it was going out for a promised rest after its battle, moved to The Citadel, Sandpit Valley, and on to Mericourt l'Abbé; thence on to Fremont (passing through Amiens), Naours, Longuevillette, Authie, and Bus les Artois; and next, instead of the longed-for rest, found itself back in the trenches again at Hebuterne, relieving the 1st Coldstream Guards!

September was spent in the Hebuterne sector, and October saw many moves. Starting with Coieneux (Basin Wood) the Battalion was at the Redan (Serre sector), Mailly-Maillet (where the church, it will be remembered, had been protected by means of fascines), Raincheval, and Acheux Wood, where the rail-head and the factory with its tall chimney were bombed heavily from the air and shelled by the German heavies. Finally, on October 30, the Battalion relieved the 2nd

Highland Light Infantry in the Redan right sub-sector, being in the trenches there when the month drew to a close.

November saw the Battalion taking its part in the Battle of Beaumont Hamel. Told by the War Diary this month's events were:

November 1.—Battalion in Redan right sub-sector.

November 2.—Battalion relieved by the 1st King's Royal Rifle Corps, and proceeded to billets at Mailly-Maillet.

November 3-4.—Battalion in billets, providing working and carrying parties.

November 5.—Battalion relieved 1st King's Royal Rifle Corps in Redan right sub-sector.

November 6.—Battalion in Redan right sub-sector.

November 7.—Battalion relieved by 24th Royal Fusiliers and proceeded to billets at Bertrancourt.

November 8-12.—Battalion in billets, providing working and carrying parties.

November 13.—Battalion left Bertrancourt at 2.10 a.m., and proceeded to Ellis Square, Fort Hoystead, and View Trench (Redan right sub-sector). "A" and "C" Companies sent at 10.10 a.m. to G.O.C. 5th Brigade at White City. These companies proceeded later to the old German front line, and at 5 p.m. "C" Company was ordered up to reinforce the 2nd Highland Light Infantry in Green Line.

"B" and "D" Companies at 7 p.m. carried the German second line. During this time, these companies were under the command of G.O.C. 8th Infantry Brigade. At 7 p.m. Battalion Headquarters moved to White City.

November 14.—1st King's Royal Rifle Corps at 3 a.m. also established Headquarters at White City. At 6 a.m. Battalion moved forward in support of 1st King's Royal Rifle Corps and 1st Royal Berks. "A" and "C" Companies proceeded to Crater Lane, and later to Wagon Road (on right). "B" and "D" Companies (on left) took up position in Lager Alley, between the Oxford and Bucks Light Infantry and the 1st Royal Berks.

November 15.—At 1 a.m. Battalion Headquarters moved from White City to Headquarters of 1st King's Royal Rifle Corps in German front line. Companies still in support of 1st King's Royal Rifle Corps and 1st Royal Berks.

November 16.—Battalion at 1 a.m. moved back to Ellis Square.

November 17.—Battalion moved to billets in Mailly-Maillet.

November 18.—Battalion moved to billets at Sarton.

November 19.—Battalion marched to billets at Gezancourt.

November 20.—Battalion in billets at Gezancourt.

November 21.—Battalion marched to billets at Candas.

November 22.—Battalion in billets at Candas.

November 23.—Battalion marched to billets at Domqueur.

November 24.—Battalion marched to billets at Gapennes.

November 25.—Battalion marched to billets at Millencourt.

November 26.—Battalion in billets at Millencourt.

November 27.—Battalion marched to billets at Oneux.

November 28-29-30.—Battalion in billets at Oneux.

The following month, December, the Battalion also spent in rest at Oneux.

1917

On January 9 a move was made from Oneux to Candas, to Beauquesne on the 11th, to Bouzincourt on the 13th, and to Aveluy on the 20th. From there it went into the trenches at Courcelette, "A" and "C" Companies being in the front line, and "B" and "D" in support.

On February 1 the Battalion moved from Courcelette to Ovillers Huts, and on the 5th went on to Senlis, moving to Wolfe Huts on the 15th, and into the line for operations a day later.

Intense cold was experienced at this time. The ground, like iron, was covered with snow. The frost was intense, one man being actually frozen stiff at his post on sentry, and drinking water carried to the front line arrived as lumps of ice, from which bits were chipped for eating.

An attack on the German trenches was made on February 17. Unluckily a day before the attack the frost gave way, a very rapid thaw set in, making No Man's Land deep and heavy with slush and mud. Moving to the attack over such ground was terrible; the objective line was reached, but the following casualties were sustained:

Officers killed	8	
" wounded	4	
" missing	1	
	—	
	13	

Other ranks killed	30
" wounded	165
" missing	32
	——
	227

The Battalion held the Red Line on February 18, and in the night was relieved and moved to Ovillers Huts again. On the 24th it moved to Bruce Huts, and on the 26th to Albert, returning to Ovillers Huts on the 27th.

March 5 found the Battalion back in the trenches at Courcel-lette, and on the 10th "D" Company cooperated with the 1st Royal Berks and the 1st King's Royal Rifle Corps in an attack on Grevillers Trench and Lady's Leg Ravine, taking the ravine, killing about 20 of the enemy, and capturing 30 men and 2 machine guns. The casualties of the company amounted to 7 other ranks killed, 26 wounded, 1 accidentally wounded, and 2 died later from their wounds.

The following day the Battalion moved to Wolfe Huts, and on the 19th to Albert again, proceeding from there to Contay, Amplier, Bon-nières, Framecourt, Aumerval, and Bailleul les Pernes.

Vimy Ridge.—From Bailleul les Pernes the Battalion moved up to Larosette, behind Vimy Ridge, ready to go in and take over a part of the Ridge after its capture in the coming battle for its possession. On the night of April 11, in a blinding snowstorm, the Battalion relieved the 1/5th Gordons on the captured Ridge, and on the 13th continued the advance to the line of the railway, captured the village of Bailleul, established a line on the enemy side of it, and sent out patrols to Oppy, which was found to be very strongly held by the enemy.

Owing to a mistaken order, one platoon of "C" Company actually advanced on Oppy to capture it, but were themselves taken prisoners after severe fighting. During this advance one 77mm., two field guns, and one 4.2 howitzer were captured, and whilst moving forward, at the Colonel's side, to the railway embankment, the Adjutant of the Battalion, Captain Lissaman, was killed by an enemy shell.

Being relieved on the 14th by the 1st Royal Berks, the Battalion moved into support and reserve lines, but on the 18th were in the trenches west of Ecurie, moving to a tent camp on the Roclincourt-Maison-Blanche road on the 22nd. Another move, to Maroeil, was made on April 23, and on the 25th the 17th Royal Fusiliers were relieved in the trenches west of Bailleul.

On April 29, at 4 a.m., "B" Company took part in an attack on

Lt.-Col. E.A. Winter, D.S.O., M.C.

Oppy by the 1st Royal Berks and the 1st King's Royal Rifle Corps, and then the Battalion moved back into reserve trenches.

On May 1 a composite battalion was formed of two companies of the 23rd Royal Fusiliers and two companies of the 1st Royal Berks, and moved forward to a position in front of Oppy to deliver an attack on the Oppy-Fresnoy line.

Attacking on March 3, Fresnoy trench was captured with between sixty and seventy prisoners and a machine gun. Heavy counter-attacks were made by the Germans during the day, and, in view of these and the retirement of the troops on the right, it became necessary to retire along Fresnoy trench. At 3.30 a.m., on the night of May 3-4, the Battalion was relieved by the 15th Warwicks, and moved back to disused enemy trenches in the Roclincourt area, the total casualties sustained being 7 officers and 122 other ranks.

On May 5 Lieutenant-Colonel Vernon having proceeded on leave, Major E.A. Winter assumed command, and on May 24 Lt.-Colonel Vernon having to report to the War Office on promotion to Brigadier-General, Major Winter was promoted Lieutenant-Colonel, and appointed to the command of the Battalion. On the same day the Battalion moved into the line again, relieving first the 1st Royal West Kents, and then the 22nd Royal Fusiliers.

June 1 saw the Battalion relieved by the 1st King's Royal Rifle Corps in the front line (Oppy-Arleux line), and moved back to Deutscher House and Thelus Wood, working parties for the front line being provided each night. On the 4th, the 22nd Royal Fusiliers came in as the relief, and the Battalion moved to St. Aubyn for rest.

This did not last long, for on June 8-9 the Battalion relieved the 1st King's Royal Rifle Corps in immediate support, Oppy-Arleux line, the casualties sustained being one other rank killed and two wounded. Then, relieving the 22nd Royal Fusiliers, the Battalion went into the front line, being relieved in turn on the night of June 13-14 by the Royal West Kents, and proceeded to Bray.

On June 20 the Battalion was taken by omnibus to Beuvry, and on the 21st relieved the 2/5th Manchester Regiment in the front line, Cambrin left sub-sector, the casualties being two other ranks killed and six wounded. A German raid on the Battalion right was repelled at 3.30 a.m. on the 27th, and the 22nd Royal Fusiliers came in as relief on the evening of that day, the Battalion proceeding to Noyelles for rest.

July opened with the Battalion training at Noyelles under company arrangements, so far as it was possible, having in view its proximity to the line and liability to observation by the enemy. On July 3 the Battalion went into the front line, Cambrin left sub-sector. Six days later it went into support with headquarters at Annequin.

July 5 saw the Battalion, less two companies, in the Cambrin left sub-sector front line, Major N.A. Lewis assuming command in the trenches, with 100 Corps cyclists attached, while Lieutenant-Colonel Winter remained at Annequin for the purpose of training "C" and "D" Companies for a raid.

About 3.30 a.m. an enemy raiding party, about fifteen strong, entered the front line, wounding and carrying off one man. Bombing parties at once bombed along the trench, driving the raiders out, who came under Lewis gun and rifle fire both on entering and leaving their objective. On returning to their own lines they left our wounded man, who was brought in. The body of one of the enemy was found in No Man's Land, but a complete search could not be made owing to the light. At night, however, a patrol went out and brought in the body of the dead German. Other bodies had apparently been dragged back to the enemy trenches. Our casualties were only four wounded.

On July 20, at 10.30 p.m., a raiding party, consisting of two officers and about a hundred other ranks, crossed to the enemy's front and support lines, the object being the capture of these two lines, the infliction of loss on the enemy, and the securing of prisoners and identifications. The raid was preceded by a hurricane barrage from our artillery, Stokes' mortars, and machine guns, being also accompanied with a discharge from oil projectors.

Very few of the enemy were found in the front and support lines, but small parties who were in dug-outs were bombed. Five of the enemy were also bayoneted in a communication trench. The main garrisons of the lines had apparently retired, and no prisoners were taken. Our casualties during the raid were two killed, fifteen wounded, and five wounded and missing.

Then came a move into reserve at Annequin, but from the 27th the Battalion moved into the front line of the Cambrin left sub-sector again up to, and including, August 1. From then until the night of August 25 the Battalion were doing duty in the trenches and in reserve, but on the 26th was relieved by the 8th Sherwood Foresters, and moved to Oblinghem.

There training was carried on, and on September 6 the C.O., accompanied by the company commanders and specialist officers, reconnoitred the Givenchy support line. On the following day the Battalion proceeded to the village support line, no shelling being experienced during the relief of the 17th Middlesex. On September 13 the Battalion relieved the 22nd Royal Fusiliers in the Givenchy left sub-sector front line, a battalion of the Portuguese troops being attached for instruction.

Gas was projected upon the enemy on the 14th; there was no retaliation, and on the following day the Portuguese were relieved by another of their battalions.

About a hundred enemy heavy shells fell on September 16 near the right company's headquarters at Barnton Tee, Barnton Road, blowing in the trench in five places. A bombardment on the left, which commenced later, ceased on our retaliating. On September 17 the Portuguese troops left the trenches and returned to their billets, while on the night of the 18th-19th the Battalion was relieved and proceeded to Beuvry.

Training there until September 26, the Battalion then relieved the 22nd Royal Fusiliers in the Cambrin left sub-sector, and finding the enemy to be ominously quiet, a patrol was sent out to Railway Craters. On the following night eight small patrols were sent out into No Man's Land, and on the 28th two patrols reconnoitred the enemy wire. On the following day eight small patrols were established in No Man's Land to cover work in the trenches, and, ensuing upon this, the German artillery became fairly active.

A move into support, following relief, was made on September 2. On the 5th the Battalion was relieved, and the companies marched independently to the Orphanage, Bethune, then on to Raimbert, the Battalion being watched on the line of march by Generals Pereira and Kellett.

At Bourlon Wood.—Training was carried on, and on November 5 the Battalion made a move through Busnes, Merville, and the Eecke area to the Herzeele area. More training ensued, and a strong rumour was in the air that the 2nd Division was "for Italy." The Battalion was equipped up to the last button, all ranks were looking forward to a change of scenery and new phases of fighting; the medical officer lectured the Battalion on the perils to be avoided in relation to charming Italians, and spirits were high and merry.

But the first attack on Cambrai took place, and instead of going to Italy the 2nd Division was hurriedly moved south by road and rail to take over the line from troops which had conducted the attack.

On the night of November 26-27 the Battalion had reached Beaumetz-les-Cambrai, from which it was moved up to the slopes of Bourlon Wood to take over from elements of the 2/4th King's Own Yorkshire Light Infantry and the Bays. The march along the Cambrai road, across the captured Hindenburg Line, and on to the Sugar Factory will long be remembered by those who took part in it.

Again it snowed—it is curious how many important moves of the Battalion took place in a snowstorm. This time, however, it was a blessing, for it deadened the sound of moving troops, and certainly saved the Battalion being heard and shelled by the enemy.

On the line (if a few scattered posts in shell-holes can be called a line) being taken over, the Battalion at once set to work to dig itself in, profiting greatly by the recent training it had received in "intensive digging." On the left was the 1st King's Royal Rifle Corps, and on the right the 62nd Division, the battalion in support being the 1st Royal Berks. The Battalion held the line on the 27th, and on the 28th changed places with the 1st Royal Berks, going into support positions to them.

On the 30th the heavy enemy attack developed, and the Berks being hard pressed, three companies of the 23rd were moved up to their support. The enemy gained a footing in their line, and one company of the 23rd was used to counter-attack and re-establish the line, which it successfully performed.

The 17th Royal Fusiliers, on the Berks' left, having severe fighting, a section of the 23rd was sent to strengthen their posts, and help was given in supplying them with bombs and S.A.A. On the evening of December 1 the line was readjusted between the 1st Royal Berks and the 23rd Royal Fusiliers—the Berks taking the left and the 23rd the right. On the night of December 1 the position of the Battalion was: two companies and two platoons in the line; two companies, less two platoons, in support.

On the night of December 2 the unit on the right of the 23rd Royal Fusiliers pushed forward its line. In order to keep touch with them, one company from the support positions went over with them at 8.10 p.m. The advance was successful, the objective duly gained and rapidly consolidated—one prisoner and one machine gun being taken in the advance.

Then came a great disappointment to the troops who had fought so well. Further south the enemy's counter-attack had proved successful, converting the position held by the 2nd Division into a very dangerous salient, from which it was imperative to retire.

The necessary orders were issued, and at dead of night, December 4-5, the Battalion retired through Graincourt to Hermies. To cover the retirement two sections per company were left in the line with orders not to retire until just before dawn, and to spend the night in moving up and down the vacated line, firing Verey-lights and rifles to delude the enemy into thinking the line was still held.

By this ruse the Battalion was enabled to carry out the difficult operation of withdrawing in the face of the enemy without his knowledge. The sections so left behind gallantly carried out their tasks and safely rejoined the Battalion at Hermies.

From December 5 the Battalion was in support, but on the 11th it relieved the 21st Londons in the Hindenburg Line, and, after relief, marched on December 20 to Gropi Camp, where Christmas was spent in tents in the snow. In reserve until the 30th, it then relieved the 22nd Royal Fusiliers in the left canal sector (Canal du Nord) of the Hindenburg Line.

1918

On January 3 the Battalion, relieved, marched independently by companies to Barastre for Divisional rest. January 23 found them at Villers Plouich in the Vacquerie right sub-sector, the Battalion headquarters being in Farm Ravine. On February 3 they entrained on the light railway for Equancourt, where they were placed in Divisional reserve. Not much time was spent in this way, though, for on the 9th the Battalion entrained for Trescault, and proceeded from there to the Vacquerie right sub-sector, remaining in the line there until going into reserve at Equancourt again on the 15th.

On February 22 a move was made to the line again in the Vacquerie right sub-sector. On the night of March 6-7 the Battalion was relieved, and marched to Metz, where they were billeted in huts. It was impossible, however, to secure any real rest here, for the camp was shelled intermittently both during the day and the night.

The afternoon of March 12 saw the Battalion back in the trenches again at Lincoln Reserve and Midland Reserve, "D" Company being in Snap Trench. There was a heavy gas-shell bombardment by the enemy on the nights of the 12th, 13th, and 14th, the Battalion suffering heavy casualties, also intermittent shelling during the day and night, while there was, as a welcome change, a raid on the enemy front line by the Battalion on the night of March 13-14. Then came the relief of the Battalion, which marched back to Equancourt, a rest for the Battalion being absolutely necessary owing to the fact that all the remaining members were suffering from gas poisoning.

The German Offensive.—Next came the great offensive by the enemy—the time when the Germans almost thrust their way right through by force of numbers.

The first indication of the break-through which the Battalion received was enemy bullets actually falling in the camp. Every man turned out, the Battalion took up a line north of Equancourt in an attempt to hold up the advance of the enemy, patrols being sent forward into Fins, where it was found the Germans had succeeded in establishing themselves.

On the following morning an enemy attack was beaten back with heavy loss, but both its flanks being "in the air" the Battalion received orders to retire on Le Transloy. Moving though Hayettes Wood, Ytres, Bus, and Rocquigny, Le Transloy was reached late at night, where the Brigade from which it had become separated was rejoined.

Moving again before dawn, a line was taken up round Gueudecourt, which was held during the day. Making another move at dusk, a fresh line was established at Eaucourt l'Abbaye. Very heavily attacked on the following day, the Battalion was forced to fight a rearguard action, retreating through Le Sars on Pys, where another stand was made.

Again slipping back at night, a position was taken up near Beaucourt sur Ancre. From this position the Battalion again moved back and occupied the old British trenches known as White City trenches near Beaumont Hamel. In spite of many heavy enemy attacks this position was held until the Battalion was relieved by New Zealand troops.

On relief it marched out to the wood at Mailly-Maillet only four officers and seventy men strong.

Resting at Englebelmer for a day or so, it was again moved into the front line at Aveluy Wood, where a German attack was beaten off, the enemy being badly mauled. During the fighting round Gueudecourt, Brigadier-General Barnett-Barker was killed, and, as senior Colonel in the 99th Brigade, Lieutenant-Colonel Winter assumed command, the command of the 23rd Royal Fusiliers devolving upon Major Lewis.

In his anxiety to hold up the enemy for as long as possible and to get the battalion back safely to a line being formed behind him, Major

Lewis was taken prisoner at Eaucourt l'Abbaye. The command then devolved upon Captain C.H. Bowyer, who kept it until the return of Lieutenant-Colonel Winter, who rejoined the Battalion on General E. Ironside (now General Sir E. Ironside, who earned fame in Russia) taking over the Brigade.

It only remains to add that the gas casualties from March 12 onwards amounted to 11 officers and 240 other ranks, while the casualties in action from the 22nd to the 31st were:

Officers killed	1
" wounded	2
" wounded and missing	1
" missing	10
Other ranks killed	15
" wounded	59
" wounded and missing	6
" missing	210

During the early part of April the Battalion was busy in moving, being in turn in Hedeauville, Beauval, Houvin, Houvigneul, Ivergny, Coullemont, La Cauchie, and on the 14th relieved the 1st Coldstream Guards in Brigade Reserve in front of Blaireville. Two days later it was in the front line, right sub-sector, in front of Adinfer, doing alternate front line and support duty until the end of the month.

It was not until May 12 that the Battalion marched back to billets at Berles au Bois, where training was carried on until June 7. On that date it relieved the 1st Grenadier Guards in the Ayette left sub-sector. Relieved on the night of June 10-11, it marched back to reserve position near Monchy au Bois, going into the line again in the Ayette sector on the night of 13th-14th.

During the night of June 24-25 "A" Company carried out a raid on the enemy front line, and at 2 a.m. on the 26th "B" Company also carried out a similar operation. July came round, and on the night of the 22nd-23rd the Battalion supplied a flanking party to a raid carried out by the 1st Royal Berks. On the 30th the Battalion was in the Ayette right sub-sector, but on August 5 and August 6 there was a reorganization of the Brigade front, and it went into support.

Then came the British advance, and on the night of August 20-21 the Battalion moved up for an attack by the 3rd Army. Leading off in a dense fog, the 23rd Royal Fusiliers went over the top at Ayette, capturing Aerodrome Trench, and so clearing the way for other troops to leap-frog over them and capture Courcelles.

Moving forward again in its turn, two companies of the Battalion, under Major W.B. Cluff, captured Behagnies. On the night of August 23-24, being relieved by the Loyal North Lancs, the Battalion moved back to bivouac near Courcelles, where it remained until September 2. Moving forward on that day to Vaulx-Vraucourt, it attacked at dawn on the 3rd and reached Morchies, bivouacking near Doignes.

On the 6th-7th the Battalion took over the front line from the 1st King's Royal Rifle Corps and delivered an attack on Slag Avenue, suffering casualties of 3 officers killed and 100 other ranks killed and wounded.

Relieved on the 8th by the 52nd Light Infantry, a bivouac was made at Beaumetz-les-Cambrai, moving on the 15th to Mory. On the 27th the Battalion moved forward in support to the Brigade which was fighting its way onwards, and spent the night in the Hindenburg Support Line just west of Flesquières.

The advance continuing, the Battalion moved again at dawn on the 28th, reaching Nine Wood just west of Noyelles. From here one company was sent forward and assisted the King's Royal Rifle Corps in capturing Noyelles. Then the remainder of the Battalion moved up and took over the front line from the 1st King's Royal Rifle Corps. Attacking on the 30th, the Battalion found itself up against the strong position of Mount sur l'Ouvres, suffering casualties of two officers and sixty-four other ranks. This position could only be subsequently captured by the use of a whole new brigade for the purpose.

German Tanks Unsuccessful.—Relieved at night, the Battalion moved back to bivouac at Nine Wood. Remaining there, resting, till October 7 the Battalion moved up to east of Rumilly on the night of 7th-8th, and delivered a successful attack on Forenville at dawn on the 8th. During a counter-attack the enemy used tanks against the Battalion in an endeavour to oust it from the positions secured, but without success.

On one tank, indeed, getting close to our line an officer, Lieutenant Anderson, armed with a rifle, and accompanied by his batman, got out of the trench, went forward under heavy fire, reached the oncoming tank, hammered at its side with his rifle-butt, and called on it to surrender. The iron door opened, and out came the crew, to be escorted back in triumph as prisoners!

On the early morning of the 9th the Guards' Brigade "leap-frogged" the Battalion and continued the attack, the Battalion moving back to bivouac at Flesquières. Remaining there for a few days, a move was made on the 13th to keep in touch with the general advance, Wambaix being reached after a long march.

Training was carried out here until the 19th, when the Battalion marched to Boussières. At midnight on October 22, under the command of Major H.P. Rogers, it moved up to St. Python, and on the 23rd to Escarmain, taking over the front line from the 52nd Light Infantry. At dawn on the 24th it attacked and captured Ruesnes, and established a line of outposts on the railway beyond. This was the last actual fighting done by the Battalion. Relieved on the 26th by the 7th King's Shropshire Light Infantry, it moved back into reserve.

With the signing of the Armistice came a welcome change. Duty was relaxed so far as was possible, and the Battalion employed the rest of the year in fitting itself out, and getting back into something approaching its old condition, and marching into Germany, a distance of 200 miles.

1919

January found the Battalion in billets at Niederaussem, forming part of the British Army of Occupation in Germany. Training was still being carried on, however, but sport was not lost sight of. There were platoon football matches, whist drives, paper-chases, and so on, while there was also voluntary educational training in such things as English, French, and shorthand.

On January 24 came the presentation of the King's Colour to the Battalion by Major-General Pereira. Later, on the reorganization of Divisions taking place, the Battalion on February 27 left the 99th Brigade, 2nd Division, in which it had served so long, proceeded by rail through Cologne to Ehreshoven, joined the London Division, and took over the outposts of the Occupied Zone at Lindlar on March 18.

On April 15, the Battalion then being back in Cologne, the command was taken over by Brevet Lieutenant-Colonel L.F. Ashburner, M.V.O., D.S.O., Lieutenant-Colonel Winter being appointed to the command of the British Camp at Antwerp. On May 6 the Battalion was inspected and complimented by General Sir William Robertson, G.C.B., K.C.V.O., D.S.O., Commander-in-Chief British Army of the Rhine.

In the event of the non-acceptance of the Peace Terms by Germany, preparations were made between June 8 and June 19 for an advance, but the orders on June 20 were held in abeyance and subsequently cancelled.

On June 22, at the Brigade swimming gala, the Battalion won two-thirds of the prizes put up for competition, although they had previously lost (2-1) in the "Kalk" football cup final to the 57th Siege Battery.

Battalion sports were held at Klef, near Vilkerath, on July 19, the championship being annexed by "C" Company. A competition for the best company in the Division was won by "D" Company, who were subsequently called upon to furnish a guard of honour on the occasion of the visit of the Army Council to Cologne.

The Battalion also scored in another way, for on August 1 the War Savings results for July were announced. The amount subscribed by the 23rd Royal Fusiliers was £1,137 19s. 1d., the percentage of members being 51 per cent, of the Battalion strength, and the Battalion being top of the VIth Corps list for the amount subscribed.

Finally, the 23rd (Service) Battalion Royal Fusiliers (1st Sportsman's) ceased to exist in March, 1920, after having had a longer life than any other Service Battalion of the Royal Fusiliers.

Presentation of Colours: Niederaussem, Germany, June 24th, 1919.

Great Work Accomplished

From the official narratives available it is possible to amplify, in some few instances, the great work accomplished by the Battalion, and which is told but tersely in the War Diary from which the previous pages have been collated.

Taking May 3, 1917, as an instance, when the 23rd Royal Fusiliers formed a part of the attacking force, we are told it was determined to capture—

Fresnoy Trench on a front of 1,400 yards.

Oppy Support, by a bombing attack, over a length of 200 yards.

Crucifix Lane, by a bombing attack, over a length of 200 yards.

Form a defensive front facing south on a front of 400 yards, and

Form eight strong points and four posts.

The above, it may be explained, entailed the Brigade having, on the whole, a fighting front of no fewer than 2,200 yards.

The task of the 23rd Royal Fusiliers, forming the left assaulting battalion, was to capture a certain sector of Fresnoy Trench, to form two strong points, and to form four posts....

"The whole of 'C' Battalion (the 23rd Royal Fusiliers) gained their objective, but, owing to a slight loss of direction, found the enemy still occupying Fresnoy Trench to their north.

A strong bombing party was immediately organized, the trench cleared, sixty to seventy prisoners and a machine gun captured, and touch established with the Canadians at the south end of Fresnoy Wood. At about 5.45 a.m. a strong enemy counter-attack developed from Oppy, which, coming up over Oppy Support and Crucifix Lane, and over the top by several well-covered approaches, worked its way north, and attacked the right company, whose flank was left bare owing to the retire-ment of 'B' (another) Battalion.

This attack was pushed home with the greatest energy and determination, and succeeded in driving the right two companies and part of left centre company out of Oppy Trench. At this point, however, it was brought to a halt by a strong bombing and sniping post of the 23rd Royal Fusiliers, who not only stopped it, but counter-attacked in their turn, and regained some 400 yards of the trench.

This party then halted owing to numerical weakness and lack of bombs, and retiring a short way, formed a block and a post, and occupied a shell-hole line from the first point named through the second and a little beyond it, thus forming a defensive flank in close touch with the Canadians.

This party held out all day, until relieved by the 15th Warwicks at 3.30 a.m. A strong point was also formed immediately after dark and handed over to the 15th Warwicks on relief...."

In one instance the garrison of a post calmly watched an enemy machine-gun team establish a machine gun in position; they then opened rapid fire, killed all the team, and brought in the gun....

Amongst the gallant services mentioned by Major-General Pereira in the special order of the day, dated December 17, 1917, is the following:

No. 1,079 Lance-Sergeant James Cochrane, M.M., and No. 2,852 Private Frank Hemington: In the enemy lines west of Bourlon Wood there was a derelict tank, from which enemy snipers were very active at only 70 yards from our line, causing many casualties.

On December 1, Lance-Sergeant Cochrane and Private Hemington volunteered to deal with them. Creeping out through our wire, they succeeded in reaching the tank in spite of heavy enemy fire. They put two Mills' bombs into the tank, and on the bombs exploding they came under heavy machine-gun fire, but returned in safety. No further sniping came from this tank. By their gallant work we were saved many casualties, and this daring feat cheered and encouraged the men in the line....

In the desperate fighting in March, 1918, the Battalion also distinguished itself.

"Hexham Road," says the narrative of the morning of the 25th, "where the headquarters of the 23rd Royal Fusiliers was in a dugout, had been swept by machine-gun fire all the morning, and as the Divisions on the right had retired, the 23rd Royal Fusiliers were left in a very precarious and isolated position, from which only small bodies of men were able to extricate themselves...."

Then, however, came March 28, and here our men were afforded an opportunity of getting their own back. It is with delight that we consequently read:

The old trenches were, on the whole, in surprisingly good condition, the men had ammunition and had had some sleep and food, and orders had been received that this was to be the line of resistance, and that there would be no further retirement.

It was a day of anxiety, but still a day on which our men could at last settle down to shooting down the enemy. This they did with great relish.

Bald, perhaps, these details may appear to those who have judged the war from the pen pictures of the various war correspondents, but they possess the ring of real reality to those who have known what it is to be shelled day after day and night after night in the trenches, to have advanced in the face of a rain of machine-gun bullets, or to have been forced to take shelter in an all too small shell crater, when to show an inch of head or body meant death or a serious wound.

Presentation of the King's Colour

His pride in the Battalion was expressed by Major-General C.E. Pereira, C.B., C.M.G., on the occasion of the presentation of the King's Colour at Niederaussem, Germany, on January 24, 1919.

"First of all," said Major-General Pereira, "I will tell you how highly I esteem the privilege of presenting these colours to-day.

"For two years," he went on, "I have had the honour to command the 2nd Division, and I have been proud of your work in the Field and out of it, and of the fine spirit which you have always shown.

"These colours are given you as a mark of the magnificent service you have rendered in the campaign during the last four years.

"The record of the Regiment during the whole of its service will compare with the services of any battalion in the British Army, whether in the Somme fighting, 1916, Courcelette, Vimy Ridge, and Bourlon Wood in 1917, the retirement from the Cambrai salient in March, 1918, or the recent victorious advance which culminated in the overthrow of the Germans. In all these operations, in spite of mud, heat or cold, or desperate resistance, you have always shown the dogged determination to win.

"It is a fine tribute to the British race that a newly-raised battalion, without any previous traditions, which are such assets to regular battalions, should have outfought the German battalions, trained to war for generations.

"Perhaps your finest record is that of March, 1918, when along a great part of our front detached Divisions fought their way slowly back from position to position, facing overwhelming numbers, and an enemy drunk with the idea that the final victory was theirs; it was then, when short of food, without rest, short of men, that you showed what you were made of, and after successive days of retirement you turned and held the Germans.

"It is fitting that the work of this Battalion should be crowned by the victorious march to the Rhine, and that your colours should make their first appearance in a conquered country—a country which has taken us four and a half years to reach."

"Goodbye, and Good Luck!"

Appreciation of and admiration for the Battalion was also expressed by Brigadier-General A.E. McNamara, commanding the 99th Infantry Brigade, when he bade it "goodbye and good luck" on February 25, 1919, when it left the 2nd Division to join the London Division.

"Owing to the reorganization of the Army of Occupation," he said, "the 23rd Royal Fusiliers, the oldest member of the 99th Infantry Brigade, is leaving it.

"I wish to place on record my high appreciation and admiration of the magnificent services of the Battalion while in the 99th Infantry Brigade.

"The Battalion came out to France with the 99th Infantry Brigade in November, 1915. Since then it has taken a leading part in all the many and strenuous battles in which the Brigade has been engaged. In these eventful three years we have seen together good times and bad, but whether things were good or evil the 23rd Royal Fusiliers have ever shown the same high discipline, *esprit de corps*, and indomitable spirit which eventually beat down all resistance and won the war.

"The battles of Delville Wood, Bourlon Wood, Ayette, Behagnies, Mory Copse, Canal du Nord, Forenville, and Ruesnes stand out in history as a record of the achievements of the 23rd Royal Fusiliers—a record of which the Battalion may well be proud.

"The Battalion is now going to another Brigade and another Division. I wish it the best of luck, and know it will maintain the high reputation for discipline, efficiency, and, if need be, fighting, which it has built up since its formation.

"In bidding it farewell, I wish to thank officers, N.C.O.'s, and men (including the gallant comrades who have fallen in the

BATTALION HEADQUARTERS: HORNCHURCH.

The Battalion Pierrot Troupe: Germany.

fight), for their gallant services when in the 99th Infantry Brigade. It is they who have borne the brunt of the hardships and the fighting, and it is they who have won the war.

"I cannot express how sorry I am to lose the Battalion, or how proud I am of the honour I have had of having had it under my command.

"Goodbye, and good luck!"

The Battle of Delville Wood

To the personal side of the late war we have, in a measure, been introduced by various war correspondents. But there has always been something actually lacking, and that something is the touch and the atmosphere which can only be introduced by those who have been through the baptism of blood and fire.

In the following pages the *real* touch is introduced. Every incident is told by a man who has actually seen and experienced what he describes. These incidents are in the actual words of the writers. Nothing is altered.

Here, then, is the story of the capture of Delville Wood by the 1st Sportsman's Battalion in 1916, told by Major N.A. Lewis, D.S.O., M.C.:

For two days before the fight the Battalion occupied some trenches near Bernefay Wood, and sustained a number of casualties from shell-fire. Battalion headquarters was a shelter dug in a bank at the side of Bernefay Wood. This shelter was constructed by Albany, the sculler, and as he was killed in the fight it was his last job as dug-out constructor. Needless to say, he did this job excellently.

For some hours before the Battalion moved off to take up its position, the Huns shelled the area with gas shells. Fortunately, however, just before 11 p.m., the time for starting, a breeze sprang up, and we were able to move without wearing gas masks.

The move up was not pleasant. The area had been much fought over, it had been impossible to bury the dead for ten days, and it was a hot July!

Our artillery was firing to cover our move up. Just after passing Longueval one of our shells dropped, unfortunately, near the platoon which, with the C.O., I was following. As luck would have it, though, only one man was badly wounded. The platoon, of course, went on, and the C.O. went over to the man who had been hit.

'It's hard lines, sir,' said the man.

'I know it is,' said the C.O., 'but you will soon be all right. The stretcher-bearers are coming.'

'Oh, it's not that,' was the man's rejoinder. 'It's being hit now! Here have I been all this time in France without having a real go at the b——s, and now the chance has come, here I go and get knocked out.'

The C.O. made only one remark to me as we passed on. It was: 'Well, if that's what the rest of the Battalion feels, I have no fears for tomorrow.'

We took up our position in a trench at the edge of the wood. This was all that remained after the South Africans had been beaten back, and our attack was to start at dawn on the following morning. This attack was in two parts, two companies to take the first objective, a trench in the centre of the wood, and two companies to capture the far edge, and dig themselves in there. The 1/60th were on our right, each battalion having half the wood allotted to it.

The waves formed up in position shortly before dawn, and it was our first experience of going over the top as a battalion. The men, however, were quite cool and cheerful; in fact, one, named Lewis Turner, asked me, 'How long to go?' I looked at my watch, and said, 'Five minutes.' His reply was, 'Oh, then I've time to finish my breakfast.' And he did.

At zero our barrage started, and our first waves were off, the thing I noticed most being that most of the men were smokin g as they went over. The whole wood was immediately full of machine-gun bullets. There must have been hundreds of machine guns—up in trees, hidden in the undergrowth, in fact all over the place. The Hun artillery came down on all the approaches to the wood, but not on the wood itself so long as any of their own men were in it.

Owing to the position of the wood, however, at the apex of a captured triangle of ground, we received fire from both flanks, and also from our right rear, as well as from the front.

The first objective was quickly taken, and then there was a

pause before the advance to the second. A large number of prisoners came in, and were herded up near Battalion headquarters' trench. We then found that we were up against the Brandenburg Regiment, which had been specially sent up to hold the wood.

A number of these prisoners next got into a shell-hole near Battalion headquarters, refusing to come farther, and one of the funniest sights was to see our R.S.M., Sergeant-Major Powney, who, as a rule, was most dignified, rush at them, and kick and cuff them out of it.

I said to him: 'Sergeant-Major, that's not your job.' He replied: 'I know that, sir, but I couldn't help it.' Poor Powney was wounded later in the day, and died of his wounds.

The advance to the second objective started promptly, but the Hun fought hard for a time, and held us up. Every bush seemed to contain a machine gun, and a redoubt on our left front caused us many casualties. This redoubt contained several machine guns, with overhead cover, and a first-aid post. As soon as the C.O. received news of this check he sent up two reserve Lewis guns. These worked round the redoubt, and, finding an opening, killed most of the garrison, and then rushed it. The survivors fled, but Sergeant Royston found one of their own guns was still in action, and finished them off with it.

Dealing With Counter-Attacks.—The final objective was quickly reached and consolidated, and for a while our men had a pleasant time dealing with counter-attacks from the front. The field of fire was good, and they quickly dealt with all the attempts made to push us back. Our casualties, though, were very heavy, particularly amongst officers. At one time 'A' Company was commanded by Lance-Corporal Goodman, and another company by a C.S.M.

Then the Hun artillery got busy on the wood, which was, of course, an ideal mark. For the rest of the day they simply poured heavy shells in. It was pretty terrible. Trees were torn up by the dozens, and fell blazing. By the end of the day there was nothing but shattered stumps.

The Medical Officer had a busy time, and owing to the barrage could not evacuate his wounded. The aid post was filled, and the overflow had to be put in shell-holes round about. The consequence was that many of them were killed as they lay there. Owing to the barrage, too, the sending of messages back to Brigade headquarters and the companies in front became almost impossible. Out of sixteen headquarter runners no fewer than fourteen became casualties before mid-day.

One message was sent back by carrier pigeon, and a message received from the Brigadier read: 'Hold on. Reinforcements are being sent.' The reply of the C.O. was: 'Of course we shall hold on. We are being hammered, but our tails are still up.'

As the day wore on many efforts were made to get round our flanks and turn us out. Bombing parties crept up, and had to be dealt with by our bombers. It was in one of these tussles that Jerry Delany (the famous boxer) was killed.

At one time word came from our comrades on the right that the Hun had broken through. So we sent over a party to their assistance, and finally repelled the attackers. We spent the whole of the afternoon and evening in this way, but when our relief came up that night we handed over the wood intact.

The scene at night was awful, the wood being ablaze in many places. I read messages and wrote out the relief orders by the light of a blazing tree, which had fallen across the shell-hole then being occupied by Battalion headquarters.

During the night our Brigadier came up and held a conference in our shell-hole. One of our men, Corporal Walker, who was attached to the Brigade Machine-Gun Company, came to this conference, and when asked by the Brigadier what he wanted, replied: 'I have reason to believe, sir, I now command the Machine-Gun Company.' This was actually the case, and he brought the remnants out, being badly wounded in doing so.

We were relieved by the 6th Brigade, and at dawn returned to our quarters at Bernefay—that is to say, those of us who were left. Our casualties were nearly 400, over 60 per cent, of those who went in. Out of eighteen officers who went into the wood, thirteen became casualties, every company commander being included in this number, while the 1/60th suffered equally heavily.

As I was making out our casualty return in our headquarters' shell-hole by the light of the blazing trees, our Quartermaster appeared with the rations. He threw a newspaper down to me, with the remark: 'You'll find something interesting in that.' I opened the paper, and found a full column describing how the

South Africans took Delville Wood!

When we were moving back into support, I noticed a horrible smell, and found it was due to the fact that almost every man was smoking a Hun cigar, large quantities of which had been found in the trenches, together with large quantities of soda-water.

One of the Hun officer prisoners remarked that our advance through the wood was the finest thing they ever saw, but that he objected to being captured by civilians.

★ ★ ★ ★ ★

Some Lighter Stories.—Another story of Delville Wood, introducing the M.O.

During the Delville Wood show a captured Hun Red Cross man was lending a hand in the Battalion aid post. Suddenly a scuffle was heard on the steps of the dug-out, and the prisoner went to see what was the matter. 'What's happened?' asked Doc. Isaac, busily engaged in bandaging a wounded man.

'Oh, it's only some of those b—— Bosches!' was the reply....

★ ★ ★ ★ ★

There were many middle-aged men in the First Sportsman's. This introduces one of them.

The Battalion was marching down the main street of Carnoy when a charming French girl of about eighteen dashed into the line of route, evidently with the idea of 'parleyvooing' with one of the young sports. She commenced in a breezy manner chatting with my father, a youngster of fifty, not noting, at first, his grey hair. Suddenly he turned his head toward her and smiled. 'Oh, papa!' she ejaculated, and fled....

★ ★ ★ ★ ★

The quartermaster is a noted personage in the army. This is to introduce him.

While the Battalion was at Aix Neulette the transport came under shell-fire one morning. The shells came nearer and nearer, in a direct line with the water-carts, highly polished, the pride of the corporal in charge. The personnel eventually thought fit to take shelter in an adjacent shell-hole until the Hun had finished his unpleasant pranks.

Over came the fifth shell with a whistle and a scream, and—

63

bang!—up went the two carts in the air, while shell fragments flew all over the place. Hanging on a line were various articles of washing, the clean clothes of the water-cart crew. These were in the line of fire, and as a consequence were well perforated. Now comes the sequel. They were taken to the Quartermaster on the following morning, and, so it is said, he refused to replace them *on the ground that the holes were not the result of fair wear and tear!*...

★ ★ ★ ★ ★

Two gentlemen rankers are introduced here.

After some months of hard roughing it, two of the Battalion cooks decided to apply, modestly, for commissions. So they duly appeared before the Colonel. But the summons to attend did not give them time in which to get out of their cooking rig, and the sergeant paraded them in their old overalls.

'Hem. Where were you educated?' asked the Colonel of one man.

'Rugby and Oxford,' was the reply.

'And what were you in private life?' asked the Colonel, turning to the other.

'A painter.'

'A painter?' queried the Colonel.

'Yes, sir. I have exhibited at the Royal Academy....'

★ ★ ★ ★ ★

Many Germans left London when the war started, to fight against us. This is one of them, turned up as a prisoner.

We were up the line one day when a patrol brought in a Hun prisoner. Of course we wanted information, for we were expecting an attack of some sort that very night. So we hauled our man up before the C.O. and started asking him questions. We tried him in German, and got no reply. We tried French with him, and it had no result. Then, seeing he was eyeing a water-bottle eagerly, I suddenly thought he might be thirsty.

'Ask him if he would like a drink,' I suggested.

'I should,' came the reply, in quite as good English as I could have spoken myself. Naturally I was surprised, and I asked him where he had learnt his English.

'In London, sir,' was the rejoinder. 'I worked as a barber close to Holborn for years.'

We gave him a little drink of whisky, and he told us there would be no attack that night. But we took no chances. A guard, with fixed bayonet, was placed over him, and he was told in English that he would be the first to get his medicine if he had played us false.

He had not, however. No attack was made, and he was sent back behind the lines to the 'cage' next day....

★ ★ ★ ★ ★

Another.

Overheard in the ranks on the march up the Cambrai Road in a snowstorm to take over at Bourlon Wood.

"Italy!" said the Doc. "It looks more like being *another* b—— Wood!"

Experiences as a Prisoner Of War

"*Reported missing.*"

Many poignant memories attach to such a bald announcement as this. Dead—probably a prisoner of war—perhaps. And there have been those who would have preferred, had they had the chance, of a death under the open sky to imprisonment under the Hun.

In the diary of a 23rd Royal Fusilier, "Mr. Brooks, the schoolmaster," as he was once dubbed by his captors, tells the story of how he was made a prisoner, his detention by the enemy, and his eventual return home.

The arrival of a parcel, he says, was a red-letter event; the problem of how much to eat at a time, and how much to save out of his rations for the provision of another apology of a meal, was a big one. Boiled nettles and dandelions for dinner and tea on Whit Sunday, 1917, proves what the fare actually was; quarters of eggs were unaccustomed luxuries. "I have picked mouldy crusts off the ground, and prunes off dust-heaps," he says.

Dry bread and tea was a luxurious meal; beards had to be cut, or pulled out by means of borrowed scissors; one loaf, and a small one at that, had to prove sufficient for the needs of five men; there were occasional intervals of twenty-two hours between meals. "We were thinking of nothing but food," he explains. All this time, too, the prisoners were engaged in heavy manual work, humping bricks, loading and stacking hay, and so on.

While in hospital, "Mr. Brooks, the schoolmaster," sold his boots for tobacco and his socks for bread, and he mixed his jam ration with coffee in order to eke it out. "Personally, I am hungry all day long," is how he describes his feelings. "I bought about one-sixth of a loaf for seventeen cigarettes."

"I was rather slow in getting into bed," is how he describes another of his experiences, "and the German orderly picked up my satchel and hurled it against the wall, open as it was, at the risk of spilling its contents."

He pays a deep tribute to the humanity of the French who were still living in the occupied territory; the Belgians he met were also kind; some Germans showed traces of feeling, others were no better than brutes....

Here, however, are actual extracts from the diary itself. They speak for themselves.

Three or four Germans began to advance, and it seemed to me that the question which had been at the back of my mind since a second or two after the first opening of the guns, Was this the end? was about to be answered....

With many signs to hasten, my German hurried me on. Soon, with three others, I found myself by poor old Bill Shoebridge, a good old grumbler of some fifty summers, who had been cruelly sent out to us in December, and had kept his end up well, with, at times, many grumblings. He was painfully hit above the knee....

We came to the village, yet unsmashed, but showing signs that it had received a knock or two. OPPY was printed in black letters on white boards in various places, and after wondering for some time what Oppy meant I found it was the name of a place.... We were then marched off, and after some more wandering found ourselves in a kitchen with two or three Germans, who looked quite comfortable, well fed, and at home....

The Germans we saw almost all regarded us kindly, though many of them had something of mockery in their looks. We now began to see a few of the French inhabitants. They are splendid. Willingly they give us all they can spare, and much that they cannot. Were it not for the fact that they are not allowed to give, and that all their gifts have to be *sub rosa*, we should, I think, want for little....

Then came the first unpleasant incident. A poor Frenchwoman rushed out and gave a loaf to one of us. One of the guards, a boy of about nineteen, snatched it out of his hands, and threw it on the pavement in front of the woman.

At Phalemphin station we were all included in a party of eighty. We were addressed in English by a German officer. The gist of his remarks was that we were to be marched to our destination, and that any man who tried to escape would be incontinently shot, also that any man who did not behave would be punished.

After this day, Saturday, April 28, for more than five and a half weeks, day in and day out, we left our prison between 6.15 and 6.40, struck work and returned for dinner between 11.15 and 1.30, according to the job, left the prison at 1.30 (if we had not arrived for dinner until after 1 we got extra time), and struck work any time between 5.30 and 10.30. . . .

In our (British) lines if one (a prisoner of war) has to work extra time, one always gets time off to compensate, also one has plenty of food to work on. Here, extra work carried no compensations. The work, especially latterly, was mainly unloading trucks, pushing the trucks about, and packing the contents of the trucks in various stores.

In the yard were always parties of French and Belgians working, and, if allowed, they would have given us their souls. At the commencement of our stay, however, we were told to take nothing from the French, and it was certainly not many days before we found it was almost impossible to take anything from them because the penalty was so great. Whenever the French and the Belgians did get a chance they availed themselves of it....

Let us never forget that we also got things from the Germans. Until we reached Phalemphin we had received no rough or cruel treatment whatever....

At Douai our gaolers were without exception friendly and kind; at Lille our gaolers were taciturn, and when they did speak, though loud and threatening in words, laid hands on no man. We were, therefore, expecting no man-handling, and it came as a fearful shock. It is my impression that man-handling began in about four days' time, but it may be that some smaller incident, such as being thumped in the back by the guard, had passed unnoticed as being mere playfulness on their part.

As to man-handling, it began slowly and increased in frequency, and I think in severity, as the time went on, until, to me at any rate, it became somewhat of a nightmare. Within a week of our arrival at Phalemphin the guard would rush at, beat, strike, or kick any man who had a pipe or cigarette in his mouth while we were being counted in the yard. . . .

Suddenly the man in charge in that part of the yard appeared. It was the first time I had seen him. Judging from first impressions, he was a quiet, self-contained, steady kind of man, rather like the great 'Agrippa' in 'Shock-headed Peter' to look at. . . . Suddenly the man changed, and with a sudden rush was amongst us.

'Agrippa,' thinking he was being disparaged, flew at Barber and struck him violently two or three times in the face. One of our sergeants, named Morley, remonstrated, and in a second 'Agrippa' had struck him two or three times in the face. . . .

I don't know what you would think of one and a half spoonfuls of jam, or grease, or preserved meat, or half an uncooked herring for the only thing to eat daily in addition to dry bread and a bowl of soup at midday, but such are our rations, and I can tell you that by now one has got to look forward to the day's issue as a very big thing. . . .

The first 'tying up' shows him, the sergeant-major, at his best as a wise judge, jury, and executioner. . . . The method of tying up was as follows: In the garden behind our barn were some trees. The man had to stand with his feet close together and his back to the tree; he was then tied to the tree by a strap round the ankles.

His hands were tied together behind his back and the strap passed round the tree. The third strap was the worst; it was tied round the man's neck, and tied tightly round the tree, so that the back of the man's head was against the tree.

Of course, a good deal depended upon the guard—some guards would tie all the straps lightly, some would tie some men tight and others loose, and so on. The most popular tree for tying men up to was not straight, so that being tied up tightly to it was no joke, as I can vouch for. . . .

A favourite pastime of the sergeant-major was to come and watch the men at work. Then, indeed, did everyone buck up. . . . On one occasion I saw him mercilessly belabour an Australian boy with his stick. The boy had not been able to respond quickly enough to his order.

Well, it is six months tomorrow since I had an English meal. (This is written in hospital.) The last three days I have tried the tip of having a drink of coffee at breakfast-time, and having my breakfast between 8.30 and 10, but I don't know that it is any better. Strange are the ways of this hospital—no soap and no clean bedding since I came in.

Sometimes peace and go as you please, sometimes every little rule fussed about. Clothes and food are not in any way satisfactory, but one is getting a rest, and that is what one should remember. . . . Suspense. Waiting with, oh, how many hopes and fears, for that parcel to turn up. Hungrier and hungrier, and with the dread of tobacco running out. . . ."

Then in conclusion comes a pathetic little personal note.

I have never read this through since I returned in December, 1918. Seeing the mention of Bull a few pages back reminds me that I afterwards heard he had died in hospital. I wrote to his wife on my return, and found she was a widow.

The Germans reported that her husband had died from wounds in Mons Hospital. I was with him all through August, and he had no wounds. I saw him in hospital in November, and he had no wounds, only boils. So I do not see how he died of wounds.

The Honours' List

THE HONOURS' LIST

OFFICERS

Rank.	Name.	Date of Award or Mention.	Decoration, etc.
Capt.	Bull, F.G.	4. 6.17	Military Cross
Capt.	Bull, F.G.	26. 7.17	Bar to M.C.
Major	Bowyer, C.H.	4. 4.17	Chevalier de la Coronne
Major	Bowyer, C.H.	13. 3.18	D.S.O.
Capt.	Barr, A.J.	11. 5.17	Military Cross
Lieut.	Colman, L.H.	9. 4.17	Mentioned in Despatches
Capt.	Gardner, A.S.	17. 4.17	Military Cross
Capt.	Humfrey, A.A.P.	13. 2.17	Military Cross
Capt.	Humfrey, A.A.P.	17. 4.17	Bar to M.C.
Capt.	Hilder, M.L.	11. 5.17	Military Cross
Capt.	Isaac, E.E. (R.A.M.C.)	20.10.16	Military Cross
Capt.	Isaac, E.E. (R.A.M.C.)	17. 4.17	Bar to M.C.
Major	Lewis, N.A.	13. 2.17	Military Cross
Major	Lewis, N.A.	17. 4.17	Bar to M.C.
Major	Lewis, N.A.	26. 7.17	D.S.O.
Major	Lewis, N.A.	7.11.17	Mentioned in Despatches
Lieut.	Moore, E.A.	22. 5.17	Mentioned in Despatches
Lieut.	Milsom, M.G.	26. 7.17	Military Cross
Capt.	Spencer, H.	15. 6.16	Mentioned in Despatches
Capt.	Spencer, H.	1. 1.17	Military Cross
Capt.	Spencer, H.	7.11.17	Mentioned in Despatches
Capt.	Spencer, H.	7. 4.18	Mentioned in Despatches
Capt.	Spencer, H.	8. 7.19	Mentioned in Despatches
Lt.-Col.	Vernon, H.A. (From 1st K.R.R. Corps)	22. 2.16	Croix de Chevalier
Lt.-Col.	Vernon, H.A. (From 1st K.R.R. Corps)	20.10.16	D.S.O.

Rank	Name	Date	Decoration, etc.
Lt.-Col.	Vernon, H.A. (From 1st K.R.R. Corps)	20.10.16	D.S.O.
Lt.-Col.	Vernon, H.A. (From 1st K.R.R. Corps)	4. 1.17	Mentioned in Despatches
Lt.-Col.	Winter, E.A.	1. 1.17	Military Cross
Lt.-Col.	Winter, E.A.	7.11.17	Mentioned in Despatches
Lt.-Col.	Winter, E.A.	1. 1.18	D.S.O.
Lt.-Col.	Winter, E.A.	23. 7.18	Bar to D.S.O.
Lt.-Col.	Winter, E.A.	8.11.18	Mentioned in Despatches
Capt.	Wiggen, R.H.	20.10.16	Military Cross
Lieut.	Anderson, J. McC.	8. 3.19	Military Cross
Lieut.	Cashman, J.	8.11.18	Mentioned in Despatches
Capt.	Cluff, W.B.	23. 7.18	Military Cross
2/Lieut.	De Ritter, J.R.	15. 2.19	Military Cross
2/Lieut.	James, C.F.	8. 3.19	Military Cross
Lieut.	Phipps, G.C.	8. 3.19	Military Cross
2/Lieut.	Bird, H. Mc.	18. 2.18	Military Cross
2/Lieut.	Brownlee. J.	18. 2.18	Military Cross
Lieut.	Carr, J.W.	3. 6.18	Military Cross
Lieut.	Carr, J. W	8.11.18	Mentioned in Despatches
2/Lieut.	Colbourne, J.	8.11.18	Mentioned in Despatches.
Lieut.	Driscoll, J.	9. 1.18	Military Cross. (Award also mention... Lon Gaz., dated 26.9.17)
Capt.	Goodman, S.T.	12. 2.18	Military Cross
A/Capt.	Gore, J.T., D.C.M., M.M.	2.12.18	Military Cross
Lieut.	Maxfield, S.C.	18. 2.18	Military Cross
2/Lieut.	McLean, A.	2.12.18	Military Cross
A/Capt.	Royston, E.	8.11.18	Mentioned in Despatches
Lieut.	Sizen, R.	18. 2.18	Military Cross
Lieut.	Sizen, R.	23. 7.18	Bar to M.C.
Lieut.	Skinner, T.E.	18. 2.18	Military Cross
Capt.	Taylor, H.A.	1. 1.18	Military Cross
2/Lieut.	Woodford, R.D.L.	8. 3.19	Military Cross
Major	Rogers, H.P.	8. 3.19	D.S.O.

N.C.O.'S AND MEN

Regtl. No.	Rank.	Name.	Date of Award or Mention.	Decoration, etc.
115	Cpl.	Albany, W.	21.10.16	Military Medal
1495	L/Cpl.	Anderson, D.	21.10.16	Military Medal
1657	Sgt.	Bell, T.T.	10.10.16	Military Medal
1657	Sgt.	Bell, T.T.	5. 1.17	Bar to M.M.
82231	Pte.	Bate, F.T.	11. 2.19	Military Medal
1375	Pte.	Beaven, F.L.	17. 4.17	Military Medal
48041	Pte.	Becks, J.W.	13. 3.18	Military Medal

88156 Old No. 1278	Cpl.	Bryden, T.	24. 4.17	Military Medal
61952	Cpl.	Buery, W. J	17. 9.17	Military Medal
4502	Pte.	Bull, W.	29. 1.19	French Croix de Guerre
4502	Pte.	Bull, W.	11. 2.19	Military Medal
1358	Sgt.	Carmichael, D.C.	10.10.16	Military Medal
1473	Pte.	Clarke, C.	21.10.16	Military Medal
20906	L/Cpl.	Carter, A.	13. 3.18	Military Medal
619	C.Q.M.S.	Catley, C.K.	18. 7.17	Military Medal
351	Sgt.	Clark, A.E.	17. 6.18	M.S. Medal
7332	L/Cpl.	Clark, E.	17. 4.17	Military Medal
7332	L/Cpl.	Clark, E.	18. 7.17	Bar to M.M.
7028	Pte.	Clark, J.G.	13. 3.18	Military Medal
1079	Sgt.	Cochrane, J.	17. 4.17	Military Medal
1079	Sgt.	Cochrane, J.	13. 3.18	Bar to M.M.
216	L/Cpl.	Collings, J.	16. 7.18	Military Medal
6025	L/Sgt.	Cornish, J.A.	18. 7.17	Military Medal
18783	Pte.	Cramb, J.J.	Not stated.	Military Medal
7613.	L/Cpl.	Crompton, J.B.	19.11.17	Military Medal
390	L/Cpl.	Crozier, F.D.	16. 7.18	Military Medal
390	L/Cpl.	Crozier, F.D.	?	Bar to M.M.
856	Pte.	Diamond, J.A.	5. 1.17	Military Medal
1861	L/Cpl.	Davies, A.E.	24. 4.17	Military Medal
1123	Cpl.	Dennis, H.G.	9. 4.17	Mentioned in Despatches
1123	Cpl.	Dennis, H.G.	18. 7.17	Military Medal
975	Sgt.	Dobinson, C.R.	18. 1.19	M.S. Medal
1405	C.Q.M.S.	Donn, R.	7.11.17	Mentioned in Despatches
1405	C.Q.M.S.	Donn, R.	17. 6.18	M.S. Medal
1649	Pte.	Dossett, H.E.	19. 9.17	Military Medal
3185	Pte.	Downing, J.T.	18. 7.17	Military Medal
48150	Cpl.	East. A.	14.12.17	Military Medal
229431	Pte.	Ervin, J.H.	16. 7.18	Military Medal
152	R.Q.M.S.	Essex, P.C.	9. 4.17	Mentioned in Despatches
4179	L/Sgt.	Fisher, E.	17. 9.17	Military Medal
74823	R.S.M.	Franey, S.H.	1. 1.19	D.C. Medal
13632	Sgt.	Freelove, W.A.	18. 7.17	Military Medal
1244	Sgt.	Goodfellow, H.	21.10.16	Military Medal
1217	Sgt.	Goodman, S.T.	20.10.16	D.C. Medal
1593	Pte.	Gardner, A.	5. 1.17	Military Medal
316	Pte.	Garratt, E.V.	21.10.16	Military Medal
1775	Sgt.	Gore, J.T.	10.10.16	Military Medal
1775	Sgt.	Gore, J.T.	17. 4.17	D.C. Medal
702	Pte.	Hopkins, H.	10.10.16	Military Medal
3796	Pte.	Hollyer, H.W.D.	5. 1.17	Military Medal
7688	Cpl.	Haslam, C.	5. 1.17	Military Medal
61752	Pte.	Gower, A.	19. 9.17	Military Medal
9635	Sgt.	Harvey, W.R.J.	17. 4.17	Military Medal
2825	Cpl.	Hemington, F.	13. 3.18	Military Medal

59592	Pte.	Hitchcock, E.J.	16. 7.18	Military Medal
113	L/Cpl.	Hope, R.	13. 3.18	Military Medal
3595	Sgt.	Horton, T.	16. 7.18	Military Medal
51156	Sgt.	Jackson, A.G.	16. 7.18	Military Medal
3419	Sgt.	Jones, C.	13. 3.18	Military Medal
4500	Pte.	Jones, F.	17. 9.17	Military Medal
4500	Pte.	Jones, F.	15. 4.18	Belgian Croix de Guerre
48325	A/C.S.M.	Jones, T.B.	18. 7.17	Military Medal
1967	L/Cpl.	King, G.W.	17. 4.17	D.C. Medal
151	Pte.	Kirby, F.D.	18. 7.17	Military Medal
3592	Pte.	Kirk, H.	14. 3.16	D.C. Medal
63095	A/Sgt.	Lawes, G.	11. 2.19	Military Medal
1257	C.S.M.	Leith, E.	16. 7.18	Military Medal
4322	Cpl.	Leveritt, H.	18. 7.17	Military Medal
646	Sgt.	Lindsay, C.W.	13. 3.18	Military Medal
57987	Pte.	Little, J.	6. 8.18	Military Medal
9172	Cpl.	Lord, B.D.	17. 4.17	Military Medal
275	C.S.M.	Lewis, R.	8. 8.16	Military Medal
275	C.S.M.	Lewis, R.	17. 4.17	Bar to M.M.
533	Sgt.	Lewis, M.	10.10.16	Military Medal
1293	L/Cpl.	Little, J.	21.10.16	Military Medal
3533	L/Sgt.	MacDonald, R.V.	26. 7.17	D.C. Medal
773	R.Q.M.S.	Madgwick, H.	17. 4.17	Military Medal
51270	Pte.	Mallon, W.J.A.	8.11.18	Mentioned in Despatches
229467	Pte	Marchbank, R.	16. 7.18	Military Medal
564	Sgt.	McCowan, T.E.	5. 1.17	Military Medal
564	Sgt.	McCowan, T.E.	26. 7.17	D.C. Medal
57184	Sgt.	McDiarmiad, J.	13. 3.18	Military Medal
1314	Sgt.	Nunn, H.E.	9. 4.17	Mentioned in Despatches
57185	Cpl.	Orme, J.	11. 2.19	Military Medal
49288	Sgt.	Parsons, J.L.	26. 7.17	D.C. Medal
357	Sgt.	Payne, E.A.	8.11.18	Mentioned in Despatches
687	L/Sgt.	Penfold, R.F.	7. 4.18	Mentioned in Despatches
269	R.S.M.	Pilkington, F.	4. 6.17	D.C. Medal
1242	Sgt.	Plummer, V.	13. 3.18	Military Medal
1242	Sgt.	Plummer, V.	16. 7.18	Bar to M.M.
57350	Sgt.	Purgavie, W.R.	13. 3.18	Military Medal
3826	L/Sgt.	Randall, P.T.	18. 7.17	Military Medal
1024	Pte.	Rhodes, L.M.L.	21.10.16	Military Medal
89197	Pte.	Raymond, F.	17. 6.18	M.S. Medal
7896	C.Q.M.S.	Read, F.C.	17. 6.18	M.S. Medal
1997	Sgt.	Reynolds, R.	17. 4.17	Military Medal
12463	L/Sgt.	Rowley, E.G.	24. 4.17	Military Medal
375	Sgt.	Royston, E.	9. 4.17	Mentioned in Despatches
375	Sgt.	Royston, E.	26. 5.17	Italian Bronze Medal for Military Valour
1719	C.S.M.	Rutherford, P.J.	16. 2.17	Military Medal
1340	L/Cpl.	Sutherland, W.L.	21.10.16	Military Medal
4680	Pte.	Sears, H.R.	21.10.16	Military Medal
1258	Sgt.	Sadd. C.W.H.	17. 4.17	D.C. Medal

2337	Q.M.S.	Sarginson, R.H.	1. 1.18	M.S. Medal
7964	Pte.	Saxton, J.B.	19.11.17	Military Medal
7964	Pte.	Saxton, J.B.	11. 2.19	Bar to M.M.
7415	Sgt.	Shepard, H.	13. 3.18	Military Medal
63073	L/Cpl.	Smith, A.	13. 3.18	Military Medal
60911	Pte.	Sparrowhawk, A.	16. 7.18	Military Medal
1318	Sgt.	Spowage, P.H.	16. 7.18	Military Medal
1618	A/R.S.M.	Stafford, W.D.	1. 1.18	M.S. Medal
1618	A/R.S.M.	Stafford, W.D.	3. 9.18	D.C. Medal
1398	Sgt.	Steggal, R.F.	11. 5.17	D.C. Medal
49304	Sgt.	Stirrups, A.T.	17. 4.17	Military Medal
1296	Pte.	Thomas, T.W.	5. 1.17	Military Medal
4109	L/Cpl.	Thomas, A.	17. 4.17	Military Medal
48089				
	Cpl.	Thompson, P.	11. 2.19	Military Medal
4114	Sgt.	Walters, T.S.	11. 2.19	Military Medal
183	Cpl.	Webber, A.E.	18. 1.19	M.S. Medal
8736	Cpl.	Webster, R.G.	26. 4.17	Military Medal
8736	Cpl.	Webster, R.G.	18. 7.17	Bar to M.M.
12315	Sgt.	Weller, C.	17. 9.17	Military Medal
60918	L/Cpl.	Weston, A.	11. 2.19	Military Medal
5915	C.S.M.	Wheeler, F.E.	7.11.17	Mentioned in Despatches
5915	C.S.M.	Wheeler, F.E.	1. 5.18	D.C. Medal
49479	Pte.	White, C.	18. 7.17	Military Medal
1795	Pte.	Wilks, E.L.	17. 4.17	Military Medal
186	Sgt.	Wingate, T.C.	17. 4.17	Military Medal
1886	Sgt.	Wood, W.F.	24. 4.17	Military Medal
1441	A/C.S.M.	Woodward, E.M.M.	15.11.18	D.C. Medal
14681	Sgt.	Wren, H.G.	16. 7.18	Military Medal
211	Cpl.	Wright, T.H.	13. 3.18	Military Medal
4127	L/Cpl.	Walker, V.D.	21.10.16	Military Medal
165	Sgt.	Woollett, C.	10.10.16	Military Medal
569	L/Cpl.	White, W.H.	5. 1.17	Military Medal

The Roll of Honour

OFFICERS AND OTHER RANKS WHO DIED

THAT ENGLAND MIGHT LIVE

THE ROLL OF HONOUR

OFFICERS

Rank.	Name.	Date of Death.	Remarks.
Lieut.	Aris, T.A.	16. 4.17	——
2/Lieut.	Bushell, R.H.C.	27. 7.16	——
Lieut.	Carpenter, C.	17. 2.17	——
2/Lieut.	Chubb, T.	17. 2.17	——
2/Lieut.	De Beck, G.C.	18. 2.17	——
2/Lieut.	Green, L.A.	13.11.16	——
Capt.	Hayward, C.B.	27. 7.16	——
Capt.	Hilder, M.L.	3. 5.17	——
Capt.	Johnson, R.D.	6. 7.16	——
2/Lieut.	Kentfield, E.N.	17. 2.17	——
Capt.	Lissaman, A.J.	13. 4.17	——
2/Lieut.	Morris, R.M.	17. 2.17	——
2/Lieut.	Oliver, E.A.	27. 7.16	——
Capt.	Ranken, D.C.	27. 7.16	——
Capt.	Rattray, D.L.	17. 2.17	——
2/Lieut.	Symonds, A.	17. 2.17	——
2/Lieut.	Taylor, E.F.H.	27. 7.17	——
Capt.	Wiggen, R.H.	17. 2.17	——
2/Lieut.	Balbirnie, J.V.E.	7. 9.18	——
2/Lieut.	Burgess, R.C.	3. 5.17	Missing 3.5.17. Death accepted as having occurred on or since 3.5.17, on lapse of time.
2/Lieut.	Cornes, H.P.G.	27. 9.17	——
A/Capt.	Coull, J.F.	30. 9.18	——
2/Lieut.	Davies, D.F.	15. 4.18	——
2/Lieut.	Dixon, R.E.L.	8. 5.18	——
2/Lieut.	Freeston, C.A.E.	25. 3.18	Reported wd. and missing 25.3.18. Death accepted as having occurred on or since.

76

Rank	Name	Date	Remarks
Capt.	Fugeman, W.A.	1.12.17	——
2/Lieut	Jackson, A.R.	25. 4.18	——
2/Lieut.	Jackson, W.	30. 9.18	——
2/Lieut.	Pratt, W.G.J.	28. 9.17	——
2/Lieut.	Sanders, F.J.	6. 8.18	Died of wds. at 3 Can. St. Hosp.
2/Lieut.	Smith, A.W.	7. 9.18	——
2/Lieut.	Wells, F.B.	10.10.18	Died of wds. at 46 C.C.S.

N.C.O.'s AND MEN

Regtl. No.	Rank.	Name.	Date of Death.	Remarks.
115	Cpl.	Albany, W.	2. 8.16	Died of wds. 5 C.C.S.
4197	L/Cpl.	Arnold, E.L.	13.11.16	——
4429	Pte.	Ayers, E.R.	27. 7.16	——
7111	Pte.	Allison, G.	1. 8.16	Died of wds. 21 C.C.S.
2409	Pte.	Alcock, C.J.	27. 7.16	——
10689	L/Cpl.	Anthony, G.C.	16. 9.16	——
1208	Pte.	Baker, G.F.	13.11.16	Died of wounds at K.R.R. Aid Post.
1585	L/Cpl.	Barrett, T.	13.11.16	——
1881	Pte.	Boyce, F.J.	27. 7.16	Reported wd. and missing 27.7.16. Repor amended to "Killed in Action."
3935	Pte.	Bardell, R.J.	29. 7.16	——
1585	L/Cpl.	Baker, L.F.	14. 8.16	Reported wd. 27.7.16. Trans. to U.K. Subsequently reported by W.O. as having died of wds. at Southwark Military Hosp 14.8.16.
1380	Pte.	Bell, R.	8. 2.16	——
1739	Pte.	Brown, A.E.	17. 9.16	——
1710	Pte.	Brown, G.	27. 7.16	——
1045	Pte.	Black, W.D.	1. 6.16	——
828	Pte.	Bowman, H.	1. 8.16	Died of wounds 1 S. African Gen. Hosp
1800	Pte.	Bown, H.E.	24. 1.16	——
1847	Pte.	Brewer, A.H.	25. 6.16	——
702	Pte.	Burt, T.M.	20. 3.16	——
4325	Pte.	Bradburn, W.	9. 5.16	——
4421	Pte.	Burnip, W.	27. 7.16	——
2474	Pte.	Burnie, J.G.	27. 7.16	——
2492	Pte.	Brandreth, A.K.B.	1.11.16	——
7275	Pte.	Baron. H.	27. 7.16	——
4621	Pte.	Broderick, J.A.	13.11.16	——
3949	Pte.	Brown, A.	27. 7.16	——
1998	Pte.	Burrington, P.C.	13.11.16	——
10679	Pte.	Bardsley, W.M.	13.11.16	——
13655	Pte.	Benn, E.	13.11.16	——
3779	Pte.	Britten, H.A.	13.11.16	——
1871	Pte.	Bennett. F.J.	14.11.16	——
1068	L/Cpl.	Clunas, C.	8. 2.16	——
1626	Pte.	Crone, W.C.	24. 6.16	Wd. 10.5.16. Trans. to U.K. 20.5.16. Subsequently reported "Died of wounds" Ashbourne Hosp., Sunderland, 24.6.16.

1942	Pte.	Cable, M.	14.11.16	———
1354	Pte.	Clarke, E.A.	26. 3.16	Died of wds. 1 Stat. Hosp., Rouen, 23.3.⅃
1219	L/Cpl.	Conquer, H.G.K.	21. 3.16	———
1309	L/Cpl.	Cross, W.	3. 8.16	———
796	L/Cpl.	Christophers, G.C.	27. 7.16	———
1957	L/Cpl.	Curtis, A.C.	27. 7.16	———
3756	L/Cpl.	Crokett, I.	27. 7.16	———
3868	Pte.	Carey, R.D.A.	1. 3.16	———
96	Pte.	Clarke, F.W.	12. 3.16	Died from wounds 5 Gen. Hosp., Rouen
4123	Pte.	Catlin, H.	27. 7.16	———
4318	Pte.	Crowe, R.J.	27. 7.16	———
4746	Pte.	Coffey, R.	13. 9.16	Died from wounds 100 F.A.
4736	Pte.	Cunnington, A.W.	13.11.16	———
12272	Pte.	Cook, A.E.	14.11.16	Died from wounds 14.11.16, 20 C.C.S.
	Pte.	Crickner, J.	14. 9.16	———
9877	Pte.	Alport, S.	19. 1.17	Wd. 16.9.16. Trans. to U.K. 18.9.16. Reported by W.O. as died of wounds 19, Horton C./Ldn. War Hosp., Epsom.
10669	L/Cpl.	Delaney, J.	27. 7.16	———
1431	Pte.	Dobbin, W.	27. 7.16	———
266	Pte.	Doe, H.	10. 2.16	———
4051	L/Cpl.	Dowker, F.H.	27. 7.16	———
765	Pte.	Dandy, A.J.	1.11.16	———
4370	L/Cpl.	Dimant, R.H.	27. 7.16	———
4206	Pte.	Doherty, J.H.	1. 5.16	Died of wounds 69 F.A.
4456				
4136	Pte.	Darbyshire, H.C.	27. 7.16	———
1812	Pte.	Dodman, A.	2. 8.16	Died of wds. 21 C.C.S.
161	L/Cpl.	Davidson, J.	27. 7.16	Wounded in action and missing.
4217	Pte.	Daniel, W.	30. 5.16	———
266	Sgt.	Ditzen, O.S.	27. 7.16	———
1451	Pte.	Eley, C.W.	20.12.15	Died of wounds received in action.
4514	Pte.	Erwood, F.L.	27. 7.16	———
478	Pte.	Fair, J.P.	3. 8.16	Died of wounds received in action.
1224	Pte.	Farren, J.P.	27. 7.16	———
1245	Pte.	Fay, V.T.M.	27. 7.16	———
2494	Pte.	Foster, A.J.	12. 7.16	Died of wds. 7 Gen. Hosp., Stomer.
1834	Pte.	Fowler, J.P.A.	12. 6.16	Died of wds. 6 C.C.S.
9101	Pte.	Fitton, W.	13.11.16	———
1244	Cpl.	Goodfellow, H.	1. 8.16	———
3780	Pte.	Glasgow, M.R.	27. 7.16	———
3741	Pte.	Garcia, A.R.	27. 7.16	———
51260	L/Cpl.	Grant, A.E.	13.11.16	———
504	Pte.	Hedger, C.A.	27. 7.16	———
702	Pte.	Hopkins, H.	13.11.16	———
1524	Pte.	Hodge, R.N.	27. 7.16	———
974	Sgt.	Hutchinson, D.L.	27. 7.16	———
1085	L/Cpl.	Hanbury, L.F.	27. 7.16	———
153	Sgt.	Head, P.F.	1. 8.16	Died of wds. 21 C.C.S.
225	L/Cpl.	Huntley, E.	27. 7.16	———
1740	Pte.	Harrison, H.J.	27. 7.16	———
4285	Pte.	Holmes, M.	27. 7.16	———
8943	Pte.	Harding, H.	27. 7.16	———

4690	Pte.	Harrison, F.	27. 7.16	——
348	L/Cpl.	Hendren, J.M.	27. 7.16	——
4683	Pte.	Hobden, A.G.	17.11.16	Died of wds. 3 C.C.S.
2021	Pte.	Heaton, —	14.11.16	——
10535	Pte.	Honeyman, G.S.	13.11.16	——
10664	Pte.	Hirst, J.E.	16. 9.16	——
411	Pte.	Hopkins, A.	13.11.16	——
2066	L/Cpl.	Inwood, W.S.	13.11.16	——
1735	Pte.	Johnston, W.H.	27. 7.16	——
1564	Pte.	Jones. R,	9. 5.16	Died of wds. 22 C.C.S.
1688	Pte.	Jones, W.D.P.	18.11.16	Died of wds. 3 C.C.S.
274	Pte.	Jackson, G.	27. 7.16	——
1214	L/Cpl.	Jeffreys, C.W.	21.11.16	Died of wounds 2 Stationary Hosp.
7778	Pte.	Josephs, B.	27. 7.16	——
4615	Pte.	Kelly, W.A.	27. 7.16	——
8709	Pte.	Kibble, —	24. 8.16	Died of wds. 100 F.A.
53094	Pte.	King, A.	13.11.16	——
1591	Pte.	Loveland, H.	13.11.16	——
1647	Pte.	Littman, S.	27. 7.16	——
4073	L/Cpl.	Lewis, T.	5.10.16	——
3623	Pte.	Lloyd, A.	26. 1.16	——
3894	Pte.	Lindow, W.A.	30. 4.16	——
4491	Pte.	Lynn, W.J.	27. 7.16	——
8743	Pte.	Lucas, A.	29. 5.16	Died of wds. 6 C.C.S.
7502	Pte.	Lee, J.	2. 8.16	Died of wds. 13th Corps Main Dressing Station.
4574	Pte.	Lambert, A.	13. 9.16	——
4665	Pte.	Lloyd, E.E.H.C.	13.11.16	——
291	L/Cpl.	Morgan, D.	10. 2.16	——
998	Pte.	Macpherson, J.C.B.	5. 3.16	——
1392	Pte.	McKay, A.	7. 5.16	Died of wds. 22 C.C.S.
1796	Pte.	Murray, C.F.	16. 6.16	Died of wds. 18 C.C.S.
1878	Pte.	McPhail, P.	2. 8.16	Died of wounds 13th Corps Main Dressing Station.
4015	Pte.	Monk, E.W.	12. 3.16	——
1827	Pte.	McKenzie, W.	16. 3.16	Died of wds. 5 F.A.
3528	Pte.	Moss, F.A.	27. 7.16	——
1277	Pte.	McFarlane, J.	15. 9.16	——
177	Pte.	McGregor, J.M.	10. 3.16	——
4008	Pte.	Mogford, A.C.	4. 8.16	Died of wds. 21 C.C.S.
4461	Pte.	Morris, J.	13.11.16	——
4618	Pte.	Moore, M.	13.11.16	——
1595	Pte.	Moore, A.W.N.	5.10.16	——
1930	Cpl.	Marshall, A.F.	21.11.16	Died of wds. 43 C.C.S.
1862	Pte.	Nancarrow, G.W.	8. 5.16	——
1725	Pte.	Owen, H.	13. 3.16	——
4713	Pte.	O'Brien, D.C.	15. 8.16	Wd. 27.7.16. Subsequently reported by W.O having died of wounds at Kitchener War Hospital.
426	Pte.	Palliser, A.J.B.	19.12.15	——
1575	Pte.	Pearce, F.	1.11.16	——
886	A/R.S.M.	Pouney, F.	1 8.16	Died of wounds 1 Stationary Hosp.
1458	Pte.	Purgavie, F.	1. 3.16	——
1564	L/Cpl.	Pellymainter, W.J.	13.11.16	——

807	Pte.	Perry, O.	27. 7.16	——
3907	Pte.	Parr, E.A.	10. 2.16	——
3129	Pte.	Parry-Crooke, L.W.	27. 7.16	——
10933	Pte.	Philpot, G.H.	13.11.16	——
3762	Pte.	Redwood, W.	22. 6.16	——
1746	Pte.	Rogers, B.F.	16.11.16	Died of wds. 6 F.A.
869	Pte.	Race, S.	13.11.16	——
3827	Pte.	Reeman, A.W.	10. 2.16	——
1992	L/Cpl.	Richards, E.W.	18.10.16	Died of wds. (gunshot), head (self-inflicted)
4149	Pte.	Rooney, E.	27. 7.16	——
4501	Pte.	Roe, A.E.C.	27. 7.16	——
9958	Pte.	Ramsbottom, W.	5.11.16	Died of wounds 1/3 H.F.A.
123	Pte.	Shotten, J.S.	27. 7.16	——
3560	Pte.	Simpson, C.	27. 5.16	——
1025	Sgt.	Skuse, L.N.	27. 7.16	——
954	Sgt.	Siever, E.H.P.	13.11.16	——
3629	Pte.	Schobiers, J.A.G.	27. 7.16	——
1222	L/Cpl.	Simpson, W.	27. 7.16	——
26	Pte.	Stagg, E.	21. 3.16	Died of wds. 100 F.A.
3605	L/Cpl.	Stares, J.	10. 2.16	——
1792	Pte.	Stokes, A.E.	14. 2.16	Died of wds. 1 C.C.S. Chocques.
1509	Sgt.	Simpson, J.	13.11.16	——
1756	Pte.	Smith, H.E.T.	27. 7.16	——
1345	Pte.	Suttie, W.F.	17. 3.16	Died of wds. 18 C.C.S.
4204	L/Cpl.	Smith, A.	27. 7.16	——
4163	Pte.	Scott, H.	27. 7.16	——
7719	Pte.	Swift, B.A.	13.11.16	——
4226	Pte.	Stotford, M.R.F.	27. 7.16	——
4227	Pte.	Stewart, H.	13.11.16	——
4141	Pte.	Smith, W.J.	27. 7.16	——
10934	Pte.	Smith, C.H.	21.10.16	Died of wds. 13th Corps 3 Operating Staff
1743	Cpl.	Tomalin, R.A.	27. 7.16	——
1904	Pte.	Taylor, C.W.	21. 9.16	Died of wounds (gas), 13 Staty. Hosp.
11	Sgt.	Taylor, J.H.	27. 7.16	——
68	Pte.	Thomas, T.J.	23. 3.16	Died of wds. 18 C.C.S.
4047	Pte.	Talbot, A.J.	13.11.16	——
40438	Pte.	Talbot, S.W.	27. 7.16	——
3656	Pte.	Teeling, A.	13.11.16	——
7531	Pte.	Turner, A.	8. 7.16	——
1475	Pte.	Vickery, G.H.	15. 9.16	——
4056	Pte.	Wain, G.A.	27. 7.16	——
1478	L/Cpl.	Wilson, A.V.	27. 7.16	——
902	L/Cpl.	Whitlock, A.E.	30.10.16	——
990	Pte.	Willcocks, N.	7.12.16	——
1204	Pte.	Webster, S.	13.11.16	——
1901	Pte.	White, F.C.	28. 5.16	——
299	L/Cpl.	Woodin, J.B.	27. 7.16	——
1634	L/Cpl.	Willocks, J.C.	13.11.16	——
4460	Pte.	Wade, A.	14.11.16	——
1582	Cpl.	Wright, S.C.H.	13.11.16	——
569	L/Cpl.	White, W.H.	26.11.16	Died of wounds 13 General Hospital.
4442	Pte.	Wilson, H.H.L.	15. 6.16	Died of wounds 7 General Hospital.
4275	Pte.	Wood, E.C.	27. 7.16	——
1075	Pte.	Williams, R.W.	13.11.16	——

7730	Pte.	Wilson, H.E.	27. 7.16	———
8542	Pte.	Wiseman, W.J.	14. 6.16	———
4631	Pte.	Willsher, W.A.	23. 8.16	Died of wounds 6 General Hospital.
4775	Pte.	Woodcock, J.J.	6.10.16	———
4626	Pte.	Wright, W.J.	19.11.16	Died of wds. 3 C.C.S.
61934	Pte.	Watts, G.	23. 1.17	———
75577	Pte.	Addison, F.	7. 9.18	———
9823	L/Cpl.	Aujurai, R.	3.12.17	———
1732	Pte.	Aldred, H.D.	10. 3.17	———
63117	Pte.	Amos, H.G.	20. 2.17	Died of wds. 49 C.C.S.
93338	Pte.	Andell, N.	30. 9.18	———
1692	Pte.	Anderson, W.	27. 7.16	Reported missing 27.7.16. Regarded for official purposes as having died on or sinc 27.7.16.
63057	Pte.	Andrews, G.J.	17. 2.17	Reported missing 17.2.17. Regarded for official purposes as having died on or sinc 17.2.17.
61962	Pte.	Arlidge, A.V.	3. 5.17	Reported missing 3.5.17. Regarded for official purposes a having died on or sinc 3.5.17.
1489	L/Cpl.	Arnot, G.S.	1. 6.18	Died of wds. 3 C.C.S.
75314	Pte.	Arthur, W.R.	25. 3.18	Shown on German list of dead P. of W. N further details.
60920	L/Cpl.	Ashman, L.	3. 5.17	Reported missing 3.5.17. Regarded for official purposes as having died on or since 3.5.17.
93342	Pte.	Astley, J.W.	8.10.18	———
93337	Pte.	Aston, J.T.	4. 9.18	———
48691	Pte.	Bailey, H.	11. 6.17	———
27418	Pte.	Baker, A.	7. 9.18	———
1995	Pte.	Baker, C.A.	17. 2.17	———
50785	Pte.	Baker, H.	2.12.17	———
1997	Pte.	Baker, W.	17. 2.17	———
10915	Pte.	Balmforth, J.N.	14.11.16	———
747530	L/Cpl.	Barker, A.A.	3. 5.17	———
6625	L/Cpl.	Barker, E.B.	23. 2.17	Died of wds. 3rd Can. General Hospital.
229484	C.Q.M.S.	Barnes, A.G.	31. 5.18	Died of wds. 91 F.A.
2127	L/Cpl.	Barnfather, N.C.	16. 2.17	———
61595	Pte.	Barrett, C.	3. 1.18	———
80142	Pte.	Barrett, J.E.	30. 9.18	———
4774	Pte.	Barry, K.	27. 7.16	Reported missing 2.7.16. Regarded for official purposes as having died on or since 27.7.16.
80097	Pte.	Barsby, T.N.	30. 9.18	———
49579	Pte.	Battison, C.	8. 3.17	———
4045	L/Cpl.	Bavin, W.J.	30. 1.17	———
37366	Pte.	Beales, C.E.C.	17. 2.17	———
21235	Pte.	Beamiss, T.J.	24. 8.18	———
1375	Pte.	Beaven, F.L.	17. 2.17	———
63082	Pte.	Beckett, W.	17. 2.17	———
1723	Cpl.	Bee, L.	23. 2.18	———
4744	Pte.	Bennett, J.A.	13.11.16	Wd. and reported missing 3.11.16. Rega for official purposes as having died on or since 13.11.16.
68491	Pte.	Bennett, C.R.	8. 1.18	Died from effects of lobar pneumonia.
82	Pte.	Benson, C.	11. 2.17	Died of wds. 47 C.C.S.

3888	Pte.	Bibby, C.	3. 5.17	Reported missing 3.5.17. Regarded for official purposes as having died on or since 3.5.17.
82241	Pte.	Bimpson, R.W.	25.10.18	——
275310	Pte.	Bing, W.	29.11.17	——
20696	Pte.	Blackwell, J.H.	25. 3.18	Reported missing 25.3.18. Identity disc found; death accepted.
93349	Pte.	Blyth, J.	3. 9.18	——
15015	Pte.	Bolt, A.E.	20. 7.17	Reported missing 20.7.17. Regarded for official purposes as having died on or since 20.7.17.
14570	Pte.	Bourne, W.	17. 2.17	——
13946	Pte.	Bowler, J.W.	10. 3.17	——
49310	Pte.	Boyle, E.A.	17. 2.17	——
79744	Pte.	Bradbury, C	8.10.18	——
60921	Pte.	Bradshaw, E.	24. 4.17	——
82232	Pte.	Brannagan, J.	26. 8.18	Died of wounds.
10451	Pte.	Breakley, J.O.J.	6. 4.17	Died from effects of P.O.O. (?) enteric.
6458	Pte.	Brennen, T.	7. 3.18	Died of wounds.
13729	Pte.	Brewer, G.A.	27.11.17	——
63083	Pte.	Briggs, L.G.	31. 5.18	——
106	Pte.	Bristow, S.R.	30. 1.17	——
9164	L/Cpl.	Brockley, G.	3. 5.17	Reported missing 3.5.17. Regarded for official purposes as having died on or since 3.5.17.
7513	Pte.	Brodle, C.H.	23. 7.17	——
127996	A/Cpl.	Brook, A.R.	17. 2.17	——
1513	L/Cpl.	Brown, J.	3. 5.17	Reported missing 3.5.17. Regarded for official purposes as having died on or since 3.5.17.
6428	Pte.	Buckland, A.	7. 7.17	——
50781	Pte.	Buggy, W.	1. 6.17	Died of wounds.
63120	Pte.	Bull, W.J.	24. 3.17	Died from effects of tumour of kidney (L)
20338	Pte.	Burgess, C.S.V.	28. 4.17	——
4607	Pte.	Burns, R.	27. 7.16	Reported missing 27.7.16. Regarded for official purposes as having died on or since 27.7.16.
8739	Pte.	Burton, G.G.E.	28.11.17	——
4527	Pte.	Burton, H.B.	27. 7.16	Reported missing 27.7.16. Regarded for official purposes as having died on or since 27.7.16.
4519	L/Cpl.	Bush, H.	11. 5.17	Died of wounds.
8717	Pte.	Bush, H.C.	24.10.18	Died of wounds.
61749	Pte.	Buswell, J.W.	20. 2.17	Died of wounds.
68510	Pte.	Butler, S.M.	2.12.17	——
E/2295	Pte.	Butterworth, L.G.	25. 3.18	Shown on P. of W. list of dead.
11370	Pte.	Bye, C.E.	13.11.16	——
75586	Pte.	Campbell, W.	6. 5.18	Died of wounds.
1483	Pte.	Carnochan, J.	27. 7.16	Reported wd. and missing 27.7.16. Regarded for official purposes as having died on or since 27.7.16.
11215	Pte.	Carruthers, A.J.	8.10.18	Died of wounds.
1946	Pte.	Carter, E.A.	3. 5.17	Reported missing 3.5.17. Regarded for official purposes as having died on or since 3.5.17.
4272	Pte.	Carter, H.	27. 7.16	Reported wd. and missing 27.7.16. Regarded for official purposes as having died on or since 27.7.16.
631	L/Cpl.	Chambers, H.M.	10. 3.17	——

51804	Pte.	Chilton, S.J.	17. 4.17	————
7028	Pte.	Clark, J.G.	3. 5.18	Regarded as died of wds. in War Hosp., Germany (P. of W.).
75696	L/Cpl.	Clayton, R.	7. 9.18	————
93356	Pte.	Clennel, J.	24.10.18	Died of wounds.
63124	Pte.	Cochrane, T.	17. 2.17	————
51268	Pte.	Coey, V.J.	3. 5.17	Reported missing 3.5.17. Regarded for official purposes as having died on or since 3.5.17.
62051	Pte.	Coles, G.H.	3.12.17	————
229329	Pte.	Coley, G.	23. 3.18	Reported missing 23.3.18. Shown on German list of dead Assumed as having died on or since 23.3.18.
71552	Pte.	Collett, T.A.	1. 4.18	————
3847	Pte.	Colley, T.N.	18.11.18	Died from influenza.
61640	Pte.	Collins, A.W.	17. 2.17	————
71553	Pte.	Cook, G.E.	1. 4.18	————
1413	Sgt.	Cooke, E.G.	25. 3.18	Reported missing 25.3.18. Regarded as having died on or since 25.3.18.
10159	Pte.	Cooney, T.	10. 3.17	————
60211	Sgt.	Cooper, E.R.	25. 3.18	Reported missing 25.3.18. Regarded as having died on or since 25.3.18.
229330	Pte.	Cooper, H.	18. 4.18	————
61732	Pte.	Cordell, D.	9. 3.17	Died of wounds.
6025	L/Sgt.	Cornish, J.A.	6. 3.18	————
1594	Pte.	Cotterill, H.J.	27. 7.16	Reported wd. and missing 27.7.16. Regarded as having died on or since 27.7.16.
10940	Pte.	Cotterill, W.H.	25. 3.18	————
79766	Pte.	Coupe, H.	8. 9.18	Died of wounds.
1430	L/Cpl.	Coyle, J.	14.11.16	————
61928	Pte.	Crabb, F.W.	17. 2.17	————
61967	Pte.	Cummins, P.	10. 3.17	————
1701	Pte.	Curryer, R.W.	3.12.17	————
68610	L/Cpl.	Daines, A.	28. 8.18	Died of wounds.
12713	L/Cpl.	Daniels, F.	17. 2.17	Rptd. missing 3.5.17.
1861	L/Cpl.	Davies, A.E.	3. 5.17	Regarded as having died on or since 3.5.17
859	Pte.	Davies, J.	17. 2.17	————
161	L/Cpl.	Davison, J.	27. 7.16	Reported wd. and missing 27.7.16. Regarded as having died on or since 27.7.16.
6050	Pte.	Day, J.C.	28. 1.17	————
4377	Pte.	Dean, J.	12. 4.17	————
1973	Pte.	Deares, H.	27. 7.16	Reported wd. and missing 27.7.16. Regarded as having died on or since 27.7.16.
2041	Pte.	Dearing, J.	17. 2.17	Died of wounds.
4360	Pte.	De Backer, M.H.	17. 2.17	————
61650	Pte.	Dennet, A.J.	17. 2.17	————
71565	Pte.	Dicker, A.S.	1. 4.18	————
10768	L/Cpl.	Dickerson, G.H.	8.10.18	————
23721	Pte.	Dinkell, G.E.	3. 5.17	————
93366	Pte.	Dillon, A.	30. 9.18	————
55068	Pte.	Dixie, L.	30. 9.18	————
1424	Pte.	Dodds, W.J.	30.11.17	————
245409	Pte.	Doel, G.	20.12.17	Died of wounds.
61958	Pte.	Donnan, J.P.	1.12.17	————
18944	Pte.	Donovan, J.P.	1.12.17	————
2705	Pte.	Dooley, D.	29. 4.17	Killed accidentally (fall from railway carriage).
93362	Pte.	Dooley, M.	30. 9.18	————

61649	L/Cpl.	Dossett, H.E.	1. 9.18	Died of wounds.
868	L/Cpl.	Drew, C.	20. 4.17	Wd. 12.4.17. Trans. to U.K. 16.4.17. Subsequently died of wds. on 20.4.17 at Ardmillan Aux. Military Hospital, Oswestry
41626	Pte.	Driver, E.	17. 2.17	——
75700	Pte.	Driver, W.G.	8.10.18	——
73948	Pte.	Dumont, J.	30. 9.18	——
58802	Sgt.	Dunkley, E.	26. 6.18	——
82269	Pte.	Dupre, T.D.	27. 8.18	Died of wounds.
75592	Pte.	Edwards, R.R.	8.10.18	——
4034	Pte.	Elley, C.H.	27. 7.16	Reported missing 27.7.16. Regarded as having died on or since 27.7.16.
20409	Pte.	Ellis, B.	17. 2.17	——
63080	Pte.	Emberson, C.G.	25. 3.18	——
93368	Pte.	Embleton, A.	8. 9.18	Died of wounds.
15132	L/Cpl.	Embleton, W.	8.10.18	——
75591	Pte.	Evans, G.H.	27. 3.18	Died of wounds.
22	L/Cpl.	Evans, H.	20. 2.17	Died of wounds.
7730	L/Cpl.	Evans, J.F.	2. 5.17	——
82271	L/Cpl.	Evans, T.	8.10.18	——
6071	L/Cpl.	Fadden, E.T.	29. 1.17	——
29568	Pte.	Farrow, F.	21. 2.17	Died of wounds.
87749	Pte.	Fell, H.	26.12.18	Wd. 22.8.18. Trans. to U.K. 17.9.18. Subsequently died at Military Hosp., Kirkham 26.12.18. (Prev. No. in 23/RF SP/ 4523)
54861	Pte.	Fisher, P.	17. 9.17	——
253629	L/Cpl.	Fitch, T.P.	8.10.18	——
229432	Pte.	Forbes, G.F.	3.12.17	——
1761	L/Cpl.	Ford, F.H.	13.11.16	Reported wd. and missing 13.11.16. Regarded as having died on or since 13.11.16.
6629	Pte.	Forest, J.G.	27. 7.16	Reported missing 27.7.16. Regarded as having died on or since 27.7.16.
275312	Pte.	Foster, A.	23. 3.18	Reported missing 23.3.18. Shown on German official list of dead P. of W.
24386	Pte.	Frampton, C.W.	17. 2.17	——
66879	Pte.	Fear, A.	25. 3.18	Reported missing 23.3.18. Shown on German list of dead P. of W.
13088	Cpl.	French, P.J.	7. 9.18	——
4264	Pte.	Fullarton, A.J.	27. 7.16	Reported wd. and missing 27.7.16. Regarded as having died on or since 27.7.16.
1506	Pte.	Fuller, V.H.	3. 5.17	Reported missing 3.5.17. Regarded as having died on or since 3.5.17.
70737	Pte.	Furuta, F.	8.10.18	——
93378	Pte.	Gaughan, T.	30. 9.18	——
23131	Pte.	George, J.L.	18. 2.17	Died of wounds.
86129	Pte.	George, S.G.	7. 9.18	——
64074	Pte.	Gibson, W.G.	23. 3.18	——
93374	Pte.	Gill, A.E.	8. 9.18	——
23430	L/Cpl.	Gillard, F.B.	17. 2.17	——
61643	L/Cpl.	Golds, L.H.	3. 5.17	Reported wd. and missing 3.5.17. Regarded as having died on or since 3.5.17.
29257	L/Cpl.	Good, B.	25. 3.18	Reported missing 25.3.18 Shown on German list of dead P. of W.
59649	Pte.	Goode, P.A.	21. 7.18	——
63088	Pte.	Goodrum, S.G.	3. 5.17	Reported wd. and missing 3.5.17. Regarded as having died on or since 3.5.17.
4457	Pte.	Goodway, R.W.	14. 6.18	——

4250	Pte.	Gray, R.	3. 5.17	————
75712	Pte.	Greener, C.E.	9.10.18	Died of wounds.
3725	Pte.	Greenfield, F.	17. 2.17	————
66913	Pte.	Greenwood, H.	25. 3.18	Reported missing 25.3.19. Shown on German list of dead P. of W.
66881	Pte.	Greenwood, J.W.	8.10.18	————
82280	Pte.	Greenwood, R.S.	22. 8.18	Died of wounds.
6990	Cpl.	Gregg, G.E.	3. 5.17	Reported missing 3.5.17. Regarded as having died on or since 3.5.17.
21997	Pte.	Griffiths, L.J.	8.10.18	————
80127	Pte.	Griffiths, W.G.	30. 9.18	————
8428	Pte.	Gromadzki, W.	31. 5.18	————
1706	Pte.	Grout, H.	14.11.16	————
63113	Pte.	Gunn, A.R.	17. 2.17	————
66789	Pte.	Hackett, F.G.	25. 3.18	Shown on official German list of dead. No further details. List P.M. 601. 2.1.19. Regarded for official purposes as having on or since 25.3.18.
4721	Pte.	Hague, W.	3. 5.17	————
2746	Pte.	Haines, F.P.	28.11.17	————
4923	L/Cpl.	Haigh, J.L.	21. 8.18	————
49112	Pte.	Hall, F.P.	15.11.18	Died from influenza due to exposure on military duty 15.11.18.
61663	Pte.	Hance, S.	3. 5.17	————
49639	Pte.	Harber, R.W.	13. 5.17	Missing and regarded for official purposes having died on or since 3.5.17.
3858	Pte.	Harding, C.W.	27. 7.16	Reported killed in action or died of wds. or shortly after 27.7.16.
63066	Pte.	Harman, W.J.	17. 2.17	————
15746	L/Cpl.	Harniman, R.J.	30. 1.17	————
78967	Pte.	Harper, E.	24. 8.18	————
48322	Pte.	Harrild, R.W.C.	17. 2.17	————
61921	Pte.	Harris, C.J.	17. 2.17	————
82294	Pte.	Harris, F.	28. 8.18	Died of wounds in 16 Gen. Hospital 28.8.18
7655	Pte.	Hart, J.I.	17. 4.17	————
1417	Pte.	Hart, S.	27. 7.16	Missing and regarded for official purposes having died on or since 27.7.16.
72686	Pte.	Harvey, F.	7. 9.18	Died of wds. 45 C.C.S. 7.9.18.
7688	Cpl.	Haslam, C.	29. 4.17	————
1909	L/Cpl.	Hawksworth, K.	27. 7.16	Wd. and missing 27.7.16. Regarded for official purposes as having died on or since 27.7.16.
4566	L/Cpl.	Hazelhurst, B.	16. 3.17	Died of wds. 45 C.C.S.
49642	L/Cpl.	Heath, A.	3. 5.18	Died of wounds 26 General Hospital.
93389	Pte.	Henderson, D.	1.10.18	Died of wounds.
47783	Pte.	Hickie, G.D.C.	13. 4.17	————
20352	Pte.	Hickman, A.J.	13.11.16	————
67023	Pte.	Hill, J.W.	25. 3.18	Reported missing 25.3.18. Shown on German list of dead P. of W.
1094	Pte.	Hills, P.E.	7. 6.17	Died of wounds.
66456	Pte.	Hodgetts, F.	23. 3.18	————
75704	Pte.	Hodgson, H.R.	20. 4.18	————
1049	Pte.	Hodgson, J.C.	27. 7.16	Reported wd. and missing 27.7.16. Regarded for official purposes as having died on or since 27.7.16.
1271	Cpl.	Holcombe, C.J.	23. 2.18	————
21474	Pte.	Holden, A.E.	3. 5.17	————

48063	Pte.	Holt, T.E.	23. 3.18	Reported missing 23.3.18. Shown on German list of dead P. of W. 2.1.19.
113	L/Cpl.	Hope. R.	25. 3.18	Reported wd. and missing 25.3.18. Shown German list of dead P. of W.
26412	Cpl.	Hopgood, A.E.	17. 2.17	———
19668	Pte.	Hopps, J.S.	25. 3.18	Reported missing 25.3.18. Shown on German list of dead P. of W.
63089	Pte.	Horn, A.G.	15.11.16	Died of wounds.
4193	Pte.	Horsfall, J.	3. 5.17	Reported missing 3.5.17. Regarded for official purposes as having died on or since 3.5.17.
680121	Pte.	Horton, P.S.	7. 9.18	———
4185	Pte.	Howard, F.	17. 2.17	———
42188	Pte.	Howes, E.	17. 2.17	———
61924	Pte.	Hucker, W.J.	18. 2.17	Died of wounds 47 C.C.S. 18.2.17.
1411	Pte.	Hudson, W.	27. 7.16	Missing. Regarded for official purposes having died on or since 27.7.16.
73571	Pte.	Hulkes, R.A.	23. 8.18	Died of wounds 19 C.C.S. 23.8.18.
1754	Pte.	Humphreys, A.W.	25. 3.18	Shown on P. of W. list of dead, accepted official purposes as having died on or since 25.3.18.
78978	Pte.	Hyde, V.E.	24. 8.18	———
1518	L/Cpl.	Irving, T.H.	8.10.18	———
13923	Pte.	Ivey, H.	2. 2.17	———
63091	Pte.	Ivory, F.V.	2.12.17	———
4765	Pte.	Jackson, S.S.	27. 7.16	Reported wd. and missing 27.7.16. Regarded as having died on or since 27.7.16.
63067	L/Cpl.	James, B.C.	3. 5.17	Reported missing 3.5.17. Regarded as having died on or since 3.5.17.
80171	Pte.	Jarrett, W.A.	12. 9.18	Died of wounds.
23563	Pte.	Jarvis, W.E.	17. 2.17	———
78979	Pte.	Jeffery, A.	30. 9.18	———
1818	Pte.	Jewell, J.O.	27. 7.16	Reported missing 27.7.16. Regarded as having died on or since 27.7.16.
2870	Pte.	Jinks, W.H.	3. 5.17	———
245533	Pte.	Johnson, F.	3. 5.18	Died of wounds.
17810	Pte.	Johnson, T.	17. 2.17	Reported missing 17.2.17. Regarded as having died on or since 17.2.17.
48411	Pte.	Johnson, W.J.	31. 7.17	Died of wounds.
48066	Pte.	Jolley, C.W.	23. 3.18	———
81290	Pte.	Jones, A.R.	17. 4.18	———
3419	Sgt.	Jones, C.	28. 4.18	Died of wds. whilst P. of W. in War Hospital Mons.
49364	Pte.	Jones, F.	17. 2.17	———
4500	Pte.	Jones, F.	31.12.17	———
80194	Pte.	Jones, W.	24.10.18	———
78981	Pte.	Keeping, A.W.	4.10.18	Died of wounds.
93404	Pte.	Kenny, J.	30. 9.18	———
73413	Pte.	Kiff, A.	8.10.18	———
1603	Pte.	Kildare, T.J.	27. 7.16	Reported missing 27.7.16. Regarded as having died on or since 27.7.16.
88716	Pte.	Killip, L.W.	5. 9.18	Died of wounds.
1967	L/Cpl.	King, G.W.	2. 5.17	———
93403	Pte.	Kinghorn, J.W.	7. 9.18	Died of wounds.
51284	L/Sgt.	Kirkham, J.R.	17. 2.17	———
3995	Pte.	Kirton, B.	14.11.16	———

4382	Pte.	Kitchen, H.	15. 2.17	——
661	Pte.	Knight, H.E.	27. 7.16	Reported wd. and missing 27.7.16. Regarded as having died on or since 27.7.16.
4785	Pte.	Knight, J.W.	25. 3.18	Reported missing 25.3.18. Regarded as having died on or since 25.3.18.
82314	Pte.	Lamb, G.H.	24. 8.18	Died of wounds.
1281	Sgt.	Laycock, P.G.D.	3. 5.17	Reported missing 3.5.17. Regarded as having died on or since 3.5.17.
73526	Pte.	Leach, B.H.	24. 8.18	——
24775	Pte.	Leary, R.G.	29. 9.18	Died of wounds.
1679	L/Cpl.	Lee, C.	27. 7.16	Reported missing 27.7.16. Regarded as having died on or since 27.7.16.
63494	Pte.	Lee, H.S.	7. 9.18	——
66501	L/Cpl.	Lee, J.	8. 9.18	——
61744	L/Cpl.	Leverick, A.	28. 1.17	——
3929	L/Cpl.	Lilley, S.	17. 2.17	——
3852	L/Cpl.	Line, G.E.	5.12.17	Died of wounds.
93405	Pte.	Longstaff, A.	8.10.18	Died of wounds.
62009	Pte.	Lonnen, H.	17. 2.17	——
10183	Pte.	Lupton, G.A.	17. 2.17	——
6818	Pte.	MacDonald, H.A.	20. 7.17	Shown on list of dead.
229456	L/Cpl.	Macdonald, J.	24. 3.18	Died of wounds.
1675	Pte.	MacFarlane, H.	27. 7.16	Reported wd. and missing 27.7.16. Regarded as having died on or since 27.7.16.
229377	Pte.	Macklin, R.	25. 3.18	Shown on P. of W. list of dead.
61986	Pte.	Madden, E.	29. 4.17	——
4528	Pte.	Main, R.M.	17. 2.17	——
699	Pte.	Mann, H.V.	14. 8.18	——
55240	Pte.	Mansbridge, R.	17. 1.18	Died from heart failure.
21247	Pte.	Mansfield, H.	30. 9.18	Died of wounds.
93419	Pte.	March, J.D.	8.10.18	——
46364	Pte.	Marks, J.T.	21. 7.17	Died whilst P. of W.
4279	L/Cpl.	Marshall, W.E.	14.11.16	——
15888	Cpl.	Martin, P.	3.12.17	——
229463	Pte.	Matthew, J.	28.11.17	——
26231	Pte.	Mayhew, C.K.	3. 5.17	Reported missing 3.5.17. Regarded as having died on or since 3.5.17.
69410	Pte.	Mayor, T.F.	23. 8.18	Died of wounds.
100296	Pte.	McDonnell, F.	30. 9.18	——
49276	Pte.	McGooch, J.	17. 2.17	——
1883	Pte.	McGlone, J.	25. 3.18	——
27545	Pte.	Merricks, F.	3. 5.17	Reported missing 3.5.17. Regarded as having died on or since 3.5.17.
93398	Pte.	Metcalfe, J.	8. 9.18	Died of wounds.
49778	Pte.	Mickleburgh, S.G.	17. 2.17	——
61658	Pte.	Miller, G.V.	3. 5.17	Reported missing 3.5.17. Regarded as having died on or since 3.5.17.
73173	L/Cpl.	Miller, R.	8.10.18	——
7701	Pte.	Milne, F.	27. 7.16	Reported missing 27.7.16. Regarded as having died on or since 27.7.16.
81336	Pte.	Minter, G.	8.10.18	——
49386	Pte.	Moogen, W.L.	17. 2.17	——
3844	Pte.	Morris, F.	27. 7.16	Reported missing 27.7.16. Regarded as

				having died on or since 27.7.16.
6140	L/Cpl.	Morris, H.G.	23.12.17	Died of wounds.
50280	Pte.	Morris, J.	29. 4.17	———
449	Pte.	Morrison, A.	17. 2.17	———
73408	Pte.	Mortimer, T.W.	26. 8.18	Died of gas wounds.
82329	Pte.	Mottershead, A.	31. 7.18	———
9656	Pte.	Muir, T.J.	21. 7.18	Died of wounds.
42286	Pte.	Musk, H.E.	10. 3.17	———
93397	Pte.	Myers, C.H.	7. 9.18	———
16967	Pte.	Myers, H.	20. 7.17	———
6312	Pte.	Nash, A.E.	17. 4.17	———
21620	Pte.	Neale, W.	3. 5.17	Reported missing 3.5.17. Regarded as having died on or since 3.5.17.
37362	Pte.	Neale, W.H.	27. 9.17	———
82333	Pte.	Neame, R.S.	26. 6.18	Died of wounds.
1815	Pte.	Neil, D.A.	17. 2.17	———
1645	L/Cpl.	Newman, R.G.	27. 5.17	———
446	Sgt.	Newman, T.B.	16. 5.17	Wounded in action 17.2.17. Trans. U.K. 1.3.17. Subsequently died of wounds Alexander Hosp., Cosham, 16.5.17.
42287	Pte.	Niblett, C.H.	17. 2.17	———
61747	Pte.	Nicholls, G.A.	15. 2.17	———
8003	Pte.	Nicklin, S.S.	3. 5.17	———
4387	Pte.	Norris, J.H.	1. 3.17	Died of wounds.
7911	Pte.	Norton, E.A.	8.10.18	———
78995	Pte.	Notley, F.	28. 8.18	Died of wounds.
205976	Pte.	Noyes, A.A.	30. 9.18	———
3380	Pte.	Nutt, G.	13.12.17	Died of wounds.
15208	L/Sgt.	O'Connor, F.	20. 3.17	Died of wounds.
50283	L/Cpl.	Olding, J.L.	21. 4.17	Accidentally killed by collapsed dug-out Rodincourt 21.4.17.
52159	Pte.	Oswick, W.C.	21. 2.17	Died of wounds.
1718	Sgt.	Paddon, G.W.	17. 2.17	———
3902	Pte.	Parkin, W.	27. 7.16	Reported wd. and missing, 27.7.16. Regarded as having died on or since 27.7.16.
61739	Pte.	Parsons, F.	17. 2.17	———
49288	Sgt.	Parsons, J.L.	23. 2.18	———
88698	Pte.	Parsons, W.F.	5. 9.18	Died of wounds.
87747	Pte.	Patmore, A.E.	1.10.18	Killed (S. 1).
81349	Pte.	Pearson, T.B.	6.10.18	Died of wounds.
48509	Pte.	Perkins, A.	2. 5.17	———
90174	L/Cpl.	Perrins, W.	30. 9.18	———
7507	Pte.	Petty, T.S.	18.11.18	Died from influenza. (Exposure while on military duty.)
7384	Pte.	Pickles, J.H.	18.11.18	Died from influenza. (Exposure while on military duty.)
6232	Pte.	Pilton, C.H.	31. 7.18	———
42289	Pte.	Pink, W.G.	24. 2.17	Died of wounds.
48706	Cpl.	Pittaway, T.	23-24.3.18	Reported died whilst a P. of W.
10460	Pte.	Pollard, G.	14.11.16	Reported missing 14.11.16. Regarded as having died on or since 14.11.16.
500	L/Cpl.	Pollard, W.A.	27. 7.16	Reported missing 27.7.16. Regarded as
				having died on or since 27.7.16.

1965	Pte.	Poplett, J.J.	21. 6.17	———
79395	Pte.	Porter, S.	24. 8.18	———
1414	L/Cpl.	Powell, W.F.	28. 1.17	———
64043	Pte.	Powney, A.F.	25. 3.18	Shown on P. of W. list of dead. Reported missing 25.3.18.
23332	L/Cpl.	Prangley, N.C.	17. 2.17	———
15563	Cpl.	Prescott, J.	3. 5.17	Reported missing 3.5.17. Regarded as having died on or since 3.5.17.
245380	Pte.	Price, C.	17. 4.18	———
204	L/Sgt.	Prior, F.	18. 2.17	———
27204	Pte.	Pryke, B.J.	29. 4.17	Reported missing 29.4.17. Regarded as having died on or since 29.4.17.
68772	Pte.	Quantrell, C.R.	30. 9.18	———
1656	Pte.	Rait, D.	3. 5.17	Reported missing 3.5.17. Regarded as having died on or since 3.5.17.
53091	Pte.	Randall, H.A.	7. 9.18	———
4030	Pte.	Ransley, W.J.	27. 7.16	Reported wd. and missing 27.7.16. Regarded as having died on or since 27.7.16.
2026	Pte.	Ravenhill, H.H.	10. 3.17	———
442221	Pte.	Rawlings, A.	3. 5.17	Reported missing 3.5.17. Regarded as having died on or since 3.5.17.
42292	Pte.	Reynolds, C.	10. 3.17	———
223	Sgt.	Rhodes, H.S.	3. 5.17	Reported missing 3.5.17. Regarded as having died on or since 3.5.17.
61652	Pte.	Rhodes, J.	22. 2.17	———
68774	Pte.	Rich, C.	25. 3.18	Reported missing 25.3.18. Shown on German P. of W. list of dead.
488	L/Cpl.	Riddell, M.	27. 7.16	Reported wd. and missing 27.7.16. Regarded as having died on or since 27.7.16
81143	Pte.	Rider, H.	11. 3.18	———
82349	Pte.	Ridge, R.C.	8.10.18	Reported wd. and missing 8.10.18. Regarded as having died on or since 8.10.18.
75394	Pte.	Ridgway, W.G.	9.10.18	Died of wounds.
4525	Pte.	Righton, E.D.	14.11.16	———
75645	Pte.	Riley, A.W.	24. 8.18	———
1985	Cpl.	Robbins, A.	17. 2.17	———
10899	Pte.	Roberts, E.	30. 9.18	———
4458	L/Sgt.	Roberts, H.	3. 5.17	———
48078	Pte.	Roberts, J.A.	25. 3.18	Reported missing 25.3.18. Shown on P.O. W. list of dead.
71677	Pte.	Ray, W.A.	1. 4.18	———
37794	Pte.	Rayner, A.	17. 2.17	———
8556	Pte.	Read, C.E.	17. 2.17	———
1716	Pte.	Read, E.S.	27. 7.16	———
48077	Pte.	Reed, M.R.	21. 6.17	———
856	Pte.	Reeves, H.D.	3. 7.18	To U.K. (Pleurisy.) Subsequently reported W.O. as died of sickness on 3.7.18 at War Hospital, Whitechurch.
75643	Pte.	Roberts, W.	10. 6.18	———
1471	Cpl.	Robertson, D.M.	27. 7.16	Reported wd. and missing 27.7.16. Regarded as having died on or since 27.7.16.
65829	Pte.	Robinson, R.	8.10.18	Reported missing 8.10.18. Regarded as having died on or since 8.10.18.

87457	Pte.	Rochford, H.J.	21. 8.18	——
3940	L/Cpl.	Roots, C.C.	10. 5.17	Died of wounds.
51853	Pte.	Roper, A.	13. 7.18	——
12463	L/Sgt.	Rowley, E.G.	27. 7.17	Wounded in action. Trans. to U.K. 25.7. Reported by W.O. having died of wds. Uni War Hospital, Southampton.
1773	Cpl.	Rumsey, F.G.	29. 4.17	——
32591	Pte.	Ryan, J.D.	17. 2.17	——
87275	Pte.	Sadrgove, L.S.	7. 9.18	——
7685	Pte.	Samuels, J.G.	2. 8.18	——
38690	Pte.	Sanders, E.	17. 2.17	——
52151	Pte.	Saunders, P.	20. 7.17	Reported missing and wd. 20.7.17. Regarded as having died on or since 20.7.17.
68456	L/Cpl.	Sanderson, R.	25. 3.18	Reported missing 25.3.18. Shown on P. o . W. list of dead as died 25.3.18.
228471	Pte.	Sang, W.H.	5. 3.16	Died of wds. 48 C.C.S.
61727	Pte.	Savill, A.	17. 2.17	——
49308	Pte.	Sears, H.R.	17. 2.17	——
673	Pte.	Seaward, H.	23. 2.18	——
68802	Pte.	Self, G.A.	3.12.17	——
37482	Pte.	Sewell, C.S.	30. 4.17	Died of wds. 30 C.C.S.
8143	L/Cpl.	Sexton, E.J.	2. 3.18	Reported missing. Regarded as having died on or since 2.3.18.
3379	L/Cpl.	Seymour, H.A.	19. 4.17	Died whilst P. of W. Official German list forwarded.
8141	Pte.	Shackleton, S.H.	27. 7.16	Wd. and missing. Regarded as having died on or since 27.7.16.
75649	Pte.	Sheaf, R.W.	28. 6.18	Died of wds. 28.6.18, 19 C.C.S.
10667	Pte.	Skelton, R.W.	30. 9.18	——
1325	Cpl.	Shute, W.E.	7. 9.18	——
4766	Pte.	Sibbles, O.	2. 5.18	Died of wds. 2 W.G. Hosp., Manchester England, 2.5.18.
4255	Pte.	Sidebottom, J.H.	27. 7.16	Missing. Regarded as having died on or since 27.7.16.
5726	Pte.	Simmonds, J.	7. 9.18	——
80079	Pte.	Simmonds, F.	30. 9.18	——
1612	Pte.	Simpson, A.B.	27. 7.16	Wd. and missing. Regarded as having died on or since 27.7.16.
61959	Pte.	Sinnott, P.	17. 2.17	——
73430	Pte.	Skinner, J.H.	21. 7.18	——
1335	Pte.	Slaughter, R.F.	27. 7.16	Wd. and missing. Regarded as having died on or since 27.7.16.
1080	L/Cpl.	Smith, A.H.	27. 7.16	Wd. and missing. Regarded as having died on or since 27.7.16.
46583	Pte.	Smith, F.	17. 2.17	——
1981	L/Cpl.	Smith, F.J.	27. 7.16	Wd. and missing. Regarded as having died on or since 27.7.16.
1720	Sgt.	Smith, R.	17. 2.17	——
7483	L/Cpl.	Smith, R.L.	24. 2.17	Died of wds. 11 Stat. Hospital.
3720	Pte.	Smith, S.	14.11.16	Missing. Regarded as having died on or since 14.11.16.
75655	Pte.	Smith, W.F.	22. 6.18	——
68993	Pte.	Soloman, F.	30. 9.18	K'd in action or d. of wds. received in action on or shortly after 30.9.18.

75709	Pte.	Spark, G.	19. 4.18	——
7624	Pte.	Spright, C.	19.11.18	Died from influenza and exposure while military duty.
51184	Pte.	Squirrel, E.C.	20. 2.17	Died of wds. 10 Gen. Hospital 20.2.17.
48502	Pte.	Starnes, A.E.	28. 5.17	——
61982	Pte.	Stephens, W.	15. 2.17	——
1579	L/Cpl.	Stepney, —	3. 5.17	Missing. Regarded as having died on or since 3.5.17.
229474	Pte.	Stewart, J.W.	28. 1.17	——
715755	L/Cpl.	Stone, H.P.	27. 7.16	Wd. and missing. Regarded as having died on or since 27.7.16.
4402	Pte.	Stone, W.J.	13.11.16	Wd. and missing. Regarded as having died on or since 13.11.16.
46024	Pte.	Styles, W.R.	30. 9.18	Missing. Reported killed in action or died of wounds received in action on or shortly 30.9.18.
68799	Pte.	Sutton, L.V.	23. 3.18	Died of wounds 48 C.C.S. 23.3.18.
1892	Pte.	Tapp, J.H.	17. 2.17	——
23059	Pte.	Tattersfield, A.	22. 3.18	Reported missing 22.3.18. Regarded as having died on or since 22.2.18.
61742	Pte.	Taylor, A.	15. 2.17	——
1410	Pte.	Taylor, J.	27. 7.16	——
80131	Pte.	Taylor, J.	24.10.18	——
15866	Pte.	Terry, A.E.	23. 3.18	Reported missing 23.3.18. Regarded as having died on or since 23.3.18.
75661	Pte.	Thexton, J.	22. 6.18	——
46598	Pte.	Thomas, G.H.	13. 4.17	——
1234	L/Cpl.	Thomson, W.	17. 2.17	Reported wd. and missing 17.2.17. Regarded as having died on or since 17.2.17.
3775	L/Cpl.	Thorburn, W.G.	17. 2.17	——
47981	Sgt.	Thorning, S.	20. 5.18	Died of wounds.
18569	Sgt.	Thornton, F.W.	3.12.17	——
1979	Pte.	Timmis, J.	14.11.16	Reported missing 14.11.16. Regarded as having died on or since 14.11.16.
63138	Pte.	Tinley, A.J.	17. 2.17	——
87289	Pte.	Tompkins, J.A.	8.10.18	——
80071	Pte.	Turner, F.	30. 9.18	——
3818	Pte.	Turner, H.	27. 7.16	Reported wd. and missing. Regarded as having died on or since 27.7.16.
9151	Pte.	Turner, W.	17. 2.17	——
61743	Pte.	Ury, A.F.	26. 2.17	Died of wounds.
75690	Pte.	Varley, J.W.	8.10.18	——
71842	Pte.	Walker, E.	27. 7.16	Missing. Regarded as having died on or since 27.7.16.
37418	Pte.	Walker, F.J.A.	3. 5.17	Missing. Regarded as having died on or since 3.5.17.
47826	Pte.	Walsh, J.	3. 5.17	Missing. Regarded as having died on or since 3.5.17.
76747	Pte.	Walton, H.S.	23. 9.18	Died of wounds 12 General Hospital.
80781	Pte.	Walton, L.	24. 8.18	——
21020	Pte.	Warwick, W.	25. 5.17	——
20870	Pte.	Watking, R.	17. 2.17	——
61657	Pte.	Watts, C.D.	24. 2.17	Died of wounds 45 C.C.S. 24.2.17.
1934	Pte.	Watts, G.	23. 1.17	Killed accidentally.

1765	Pte.	Weal, C.A.	5. 3.17	Died of wounds 12 Gen. Hosp. 5.3.17.
1401	Pte.	Webster, F.A.	23. 4.18	Died of wounds 3 C.C.S. 23.4.18.
51269	Pte.	Welch, J.W.	9. 5.17	Died of wounds 24 General Hospital.
61757	Pte.	Welch, P.D.	3. 5.17	——
63075	Pte.	Welham, P.	17. 2.17	——
1361	Pte.	West, E.J.	27. 7.16	Wd. and missing. Regarded as having died on or since 27.7.16.
201	L/Cpl.	West, F.	29.11.17	——
4216	L/Cpl.	West, V.J.	27. 7.16	Reported killed in action or died of wds. shortly after or on 27.7.16.
74860	Pte.	West, W.	8.10.18	——
68624	Pte.	White, A.E.	25. 3.18	Missing. Regarded as having died on or since 25.3.18.
50193	Pte.	White, B.S.	17. 2.17	——
49479	Pte.	White, C.	3. 5.17	——
62001	Pte.	White, J.	17. 2.17	——
10620	Pte.	White, G.	17. 2.17	——
63165	Pte.	Whitrick, J.	20. 4.17	Died whilst a P. of W.
1496	Pte.	Wild, A.H.	14.11.16	Missing. Regarded as having died on or since 14.11.16.
1829	Pte.	Wilkinson, H.	17. 2.17	——
52161	Pte.	Wilkinson, J.C.	17. 2.17	——
1401	Pte.	Wilkinson, J.F.	17. 2.17	——
73172	Pte.	Williamson, J.	31. 5.18	——
5966	Pte.	Willott, H.	28. 1.17	——
4209	Pte.	Wilson, A.	27. 7.16	Wd. and missing. Regarded as having died on or since 27.7.16.
245549	Pte.	Wilson, F.	18. 4.18	Died at Adv. Dressing Station, 100 F.A.
69248	Cpl.	Wilson, F.W.	23. 3.18	Shown on P. of W. list of dead. Regarded as having died 23.3.18.
186	Sgt.	Wingate, T.C.	23. 3.18	Missing. Accepted as killed on 23.3.18.
4712	L/Cpl.	Witham, D.H.	27. 6.17	Died of wds. 6 F.A.
8222	Cpl.	Wood, W.L.	1.11.18	Died from influenza 59 C.C.S.
1886	Sgt.	Wood, W.F.	19. 4.18	——
79400	Pte.	Woodier, F.	24. 8.18	——
61920	Pte.	Woods, H.H.	17. 2.17	——
68823	Pte.	Woolsey, W.	30. 9.18	Killed in action or died of wounds.
229005	Pte.	Worsnop, H.	8.10.18	Killed in action or died of wounds received in action on or shortly after 8.10.18.
2095	Cpl.	Wright, G.H.	3. 5.17	Missing. Regarded as having died on or since 3.5.17.
4380	Pte.	Wright, J.	27. 7.16	Wd. and missing. Regarded as having died on or since 27.7.16.
68825	Pte.	Wyatt, A.C.	25. 3.18	——
7350	L/Cpl.	Young, C.W.	17. 2.17	——
48101	L/Cpl.	Young, F.	30.11.17	——

The Nominal Roll

[Note.—It is regretted it has not proved practicable to compile a roll of all the officers, N.C.O.'s., and men who have served at any time in the 23rd Royal Fusiliers.]

THE NOMINAL ROLL

Colonel Viscount Maitland.
Lieut.-Col. A. St. H. Gibbons.
Major G.H.H. Richey.
Capt. W.A. Powell.
Capt. P. Suckling.
Capt. N.A.L. Cockell.
Capt. E. Cragg.
Capt. Stanley Holmes.
Capt. H.J.H. Inglis.
Capt. B.A. de Bourbel.
Capt. H.E.F. Richardson.
Capt. H.V.C. Pirie.
Lieut.-Quar. R. de Vere Stacpoole.
Lieut. H.V. Foy.
Lieut. R.N. Sealey.
Lieut. P.V. Hayes.
Lieut. H.A. Taylor.
Lieut. E.E. Isaac, R.A.M.C.
Lieut. E.A. Winter.
Lieut. E.J. Cross.
Lieut. Hon. A. Yorke.
Lieut. R.C. Hillcoat.
Lieut. J.P. Roberts.
2nd Lieut. F.H. Cox.
2nd Lieut. G. Dixon-Spain.
2nd Lieut. W.A. Rutherford.
2nd Lieut. J.J. Cameron.
2nd Lieut. P.H. Cooper.
2nd Lieut. A.C. Hobson.
2nd Lieut. N.A. Lewis.

2nd Lieut. A.G. Rees.
2nd Lieut. F.H. Brown.
2nd Lieut. A.J. Barr.
2nd Lieut. Hon. B. Yorke.
2nd Lieut. F.E. Pearson.
2nd Lieut. L.E. Eeman.
2nd Lieut. R.O. Jourdain.
2nd Lieut. N.A.L. Way.
2nd Lieut. E.V. Hine.
2nd Lieut. J.C. Fenton.
2nd Lieut. N. Firth.
2nd Lieut. C.B. Hayward.
2nd Lieut. G.R. Nicolaus.
2nd Lieut. W.J. Stevenson.
2nd Lieut. D. Godlonton.
2nd Lieut. C.R. Little.
2nd Lieut. R.M. Ritchie.
2nd Lieut. N.R. Crum-Ewing.
2nd Lieut. C.A. Moore.
2nd Lieut. D. Rattray.
2nd Lieut. L.H. Colman.
2nd Lieut. R.B. Marriott.
2nd Lieut. L.H. Bayley.
2nd Lieut. R.O. Crookes.
2nd Lieut. F.G. Bull.
2nd Lieut. Owen H. Williams.
2nd Lieut. N. Worship.
2nd Lieut. R.H. Gregg.
2nd Lieut. M. Fraser.
2nd Lieut. E.G. Hayes.

2nd Lieut. A.J.H. Kennedy.
2nd Lieut. E.F.H. Taylor.
2nd Lieut. G.C. Lovibond.

2nd Lieut. A.A. Humfrey.
2nd Lieut. F.S. Meeks.
2nd Lieut. C.W. Burgess.
2nd Lieut. P.A. Williams.

1	Mitchell, E.C.	9	Devereux, L.
2	Hyams, J.	10	Kay, C.
3	Drysdale, S.A.	11	Taylor, J.H.
4	Roberts, G.P.	12	Dunn, C.H.
5	Garnett, P.C.	13	Preece, T.C.
6	Wharton, A.S.	14	Colston, F.J.
7	Holloway, W.S.	15	Bangs, E.R.
8	Foy, H.V.	16	Headland, W.

17	Pennington, S.C.	68	Thomas, J.L.
18	Webb, A.S.	69	De Burgh Thomas, A.
19	Cobb, A.	70	Lockwood, E.H.A.
20	Andrews, W.R.	71	Hackworth, H.J.
21	Kendall, J.M.	72	Jupp, G.E.
22	Smith, S.	73	Nicholl, E.B.
23	Andrews, P.A.	74	Logan, C.
24	Drake, J.	75	Rogers, V.H.
25	Jefferson, J.	76	Hayhoe, W.H.
26	Stagg, E.	77	Tudor, H.O.
27	MacLarty, B.	78	Bovill, F.H.
28	Cadman, K.	79	Hayward, C.A.
29	Mussard, C.	80	Mattingly, S.W.
30	Ward, H.E.	81	May, H.R.
31	Lort, V.P.	82	Wheildon, F.
32	Ayres, H.S.	83	Pledge, G.T.
33	Haines, C.E.	84	Payne, H.A.
34	Phelps, J.	85	Denton, C.
35	Maynard, B.T.	86	Keevil, C.H.
36	Howe, D.H.	87	Forrester, C.
37	Wallis, W.T.	88	Hawtrey, G.H.C.
38	Sheffield, E.C.	89	Green, H.
39	Perkins, W.G.	90	Bradfield, B.W.
40	Townshend, W.S.	91	Bridger, J.B.
41	Sawden, W.W.	92	Martin, C.W.
42	Henderson, D.	93	Hardee, F.
43	Worthington, S.	94	Moir, H.A.
44	Scovell, T.S.	95	Hodgkinson, A.H.
45	Waters, F.	96	Clarke, F.W.
46	Dowsett, A.	97	Barton, M.D.
47	Aylward, C.B.	98	Bellamy, B.D.
48	Crum-Ewing, N.R.	99	Anderson, W.C.
49	De Grehl, F.S.C.	100	Wedeymeyer, P.E.
50	Leveson, W.C.	101	McNeill, J.
51	Curle, J.H.	102	Halford, A.

52	Wylie, R.E.	103	Harvey, A.G.
53	Hawkins, W.A.	104	Nash, C.H.
54	Farwell, C.W.	105	Hopkins, J.C.
55	Stone, H.P.	106	Bacchus, W.A.
56	Sullivan, E.	107	Watson, C.
57	Wood, M.	108	Steele, F.J.
58	Hepner, H.	109	Bamford, E.
59	Norman, J.C.	110	Timperley, T.L.
60	Smith, F.S.L.	111	Thunder, M.P.
61	Fraser, W.G.	112	Wadham, H.F.
62	Glendinning, G.G.	113	Makeham, E.
63	Edouin, F.	114	Aston, W.F.
64	Watts, J.G.D.	115	Albany, W.
65	Dodman, A.W.J.	116	Barff, W.H.
66	Ropner, W.	117	Wickens, E.T.
67	Crabb, L.F.J.	118	Guy, C.H.
119	Lawes, A.E.	170	Lewis, S.R.
120	Benjamin, N.H.	171	Moncrieff, J.B.
121	Storey, T.H.	172	Felton, A.H.
122	Sharland, L.J.	173	Burch, V.G.
123	Shotton, J.S.	174	Wilson, T.
124	Chester, J.	175	Rees, A.W.
125	Troup, C.L.	176	Wilkinson, D.S.
126	Carew, H.F.	177	McGregor, J.M.
127	Medland, S.C.	178	Terry, F.W.
128	Lavarack, F.S.	179	Bramley-Moore, A.
129	Lavarack, A.W.	180	Hadden, H.L.
130	Denton, A.W.	181	Muller, C.J.
131	Houlden, J.W.F.	182	Guntrip, E.
132	Millen, A.	183	Webber, A.E.
133	Campbell-Colquhoun, A.C.	184	Cordery, G.D.
134	Cooper, W.P.	185	Heathorn, A.T.
135	Hine, E.V.	186	Wingate, T.C.
136	Fordham, W.H.	187	Field, C.W.
137	Fordham, S.H.	188	Crowhurst, T.O.
138	Picken, P.W.	189	Boote, E.R.
139	Pinniger, W.L.	190	Wallace, W.J.
140	Robinson, T.H.	191	Allen, A.L.
141	Lyster, H.N.	192	Page, H.
142	Leuw, H.S.	193	Oliver, H.J.
143	Burmingham, S.H.	194	Oxberry, H.
144	Price, R.P.	195	Reeves, H.E.
145	Piachaud, G.	196	Cook, H.
146	Atkinson, W.	197	Evans, R.
147	Meeks, F.S.	198	Peddar, E.A.
148	Smith, R.	199	Haine, L.G.
149	Henri, P.R.	200	Elphicke, B.
150	Melbourne, S.W.	201	West, T.
151	Finch, M.S.	202	Lovibond, G.C.
152	Essex, P.C.	203	Ellis, T.
153	Head, P.T.	204	Hooper, H.J.

	Marquardt, —	205	McLeod, W.C.
155	Hayward, E.	206	McGregor, W.
156	Robert, C.L.	207	Purnell, J.J.
157	Archbold, T.E.	208	Rose, G.C.
158	Buxton, F.C.	209	Hooper, W.
159	Rose, E.M.	210	Waldron, E.A.
160	Goodchild, A.E.	211	Evans, J.H.
161	Davison, J.	212	Ramsden, H.C.
162	Farquhar, J.E.M.	213	De Jesse, R.
163	Pope, E.W.	214	Garner, H.W.
164	Barker-Mill, W.C.F.V.	215	Batton, W.B.
165	Woollett, C.	216	Devitt, E.L.
166	Hobson, A.C.	217	Whitewright, W. A.
167	Murray, H.F.U.T.	218	Bannatyne, D.
168	Smith, A.C.	219	Hopper, T.
169	Morton, F.	220	Metcalfe, H.M.

221	Brydon, C.J.B.	272	Brown, B.
222	Scott, H.P.	273	Bewick, J.L.
223	Rhodes, H.S.	274	Jackson, G.
224	Emery, H.D.	275	Lewis, R.
225	Huntley, E.	276	Cockell, N.A.L.
226	Darwall, J.R.	277	Chick, W.D.
227	Duncan, W.L.	278	Starkey, W.E.
228	Powell, A.	279	Hemmerde, T.W.
229	Thornber, G.R.	280	Eeman, L.E.
230	Cave, H.J.	281	Morgan, J.W.R.
231	Hignett, S.F.	282	Sikes, B.H.
232	Ward, L.	283	Pierce, P.B.
233	Holden, G.Y.	284	Gardner, A.E.
234	Barrett, J.H.	285	Gordon, G.R.
235	Woodin, W.G.	286	Ewan, F.W.
236	Watts, H.	287	Donovan, E.L.
237	Littlewort, H.C.	288	Goodard, W.D.
238	Harris, H.I.	289	Heinemann, A.B.
239	Dalyrimple, D.W.	290	Lowcock, D.R.
240	Wilson, J.A.G.	291	Morgan, J.D.
241	Richardson, H.	292	Jourdain, R.O.
242	Driver, G.D.	293	Nash, V.E.
243	Wills, C.G.	294	Moore, H.
244	Salveson, G.	295	Bragg, V.
245	Day, B.	296	Oliver, T.L.
246	Norton, C.A.	297	Barber, H.
247	Shammon, H.A.	298	Moon-Ord, G.C.
248	Prentice, G.D.	299	Woodin, J.B.
249	Haslam, E.S.	300	Franey, G.T.
250	Wright, G.F.E.	301	Neal, L.A.
251	Richards, R.	302	Franey, S.H.
252	Christie, F.	303	Ovenell, R.
253	Mackie, E.D.	304	Moxon, F.
254	Hepworth, N.	305	Rogers, F.J.C.
255	Wright, I.F.H.	306	Reeves, C.R.

	Darlington, F.L.	307	Harwood, G.
257	Brookes, C.B.	308	O'Shea, S.H.W.
258	Taylor, R.J.	309	Train, H.
259	Watts, E.M.	310	Haskew, F.J.T.
260	Forrest, A.H.W.	311	Newitt, L.D.
261	Williams, L.	312	Jervis, W.F.
262	Tireman, G.W.	313	Leigh, H.E.
263	Davey, H.B.	314	Leigh, Harold.
264	Brookshank, P.	315	Fenton, D.
265	Curran, W.	316	Garratt, E.V.
266	Dobbin, W.	317	Down, T.M.
267	Taylor, W.E.	318	Whitehead, A.E.
268	Walker, A.W.	319	Lafern, L.
269	Pilkington, F.	320	Allcroft, W.L.
270	White, A.U.	321	Prout, H.J.
271	Firth, N.	322	Parry, J.
323	Read, F.W.	374	Morris, T.C.
324	Scott, R.C.	375	Royston, E.
325	Dalrymple, H.	376	Lewis, G.S.
326	Lee, L.S.	377	Ewart, M.
327	Lawford, A.R.M.	378	Harris, F.G.
328	Ritson, B.	379	Bayley, L.H.
329	Leuty, C.L.	380	Franks, G.A.
330	Smith, S.	381	Walker, H.
331	McArdell, H.	382	Tattersall, R.R.
332	Pearson, B. Hyde-	383	Simpson, V.J.
333	Barr, A.J.	384	Greening, E.L.
334	Deacon, V.F.	385	Harper, W.G.
335	Rawling, L.J.	386	Veacock, S.J.
336	Ash, P.C.	387	Mehta, J.R.
337	Appleton, R.	388	Cox, J.H.S.
338	Jones, A.E.	389	Sheffield, E.H.
339	Oliver, E.	390	Crozier, F.D.
340	Smith, H.T.	391	Bright, M.
341	Kemp, F.	392	Davidson, T.G.
342	Sandham, A.	393	Neville, N.J.C.
343	Parks, H.	394	Marsden, E.L.
344	Stanning, J.E.	395	Freer, C.C.
345	Thompson, A.G.	396	Beard, B.F.
346	Thornley, E.P.	397	Baillon, G.W.
347	Hayes, E.G.	398	Bradley, E.
348	Hendren, J.M.	399	Gabriel, A.
349	Maw, F.D.	400	Hill, J.A.
350	Tomkins, F.O.	401	Campbell, D.
351	Clark, A.E.	402	Fowler, F.
352	Hitch, J.W.	403	Rogers, W.C.
353	Little, C.R.	404	Yorke, B.E.
354	Smith, F.E.	405	Yorke, A.
355	Beeson, W.V.	406	Gibbons, W.
356	Ringe, F.C.	407	Barker, G.
357	Payne, E.A.	408	Richards, H.B.

	Brownrigg, A.H.	409	Michie, A.
359	Lowis, G.V.	410	Webb, R.C.
360	Persee, J.D.	411	Hopkins, A.A.
361	Taylor, L.E.	412	Borwick, A.
362	Vernon, B.T.	413	Phillips, A.E.
363	Ellis, J. St. John G.	414	Heron, W.H.
364	Wright, R.	415	Baker, H.C.
365	Turnbull, J.M.	416	Blevins, F.
366	Lennep, E.V.	417	Norton, W.C.
367	Foster, W.	418	Culverhouse, R.
368	Beard, R.T.	419	Streeter, A.
369	Wyllie, J.A.	420	Bolton, E.T.
370	Williams, J.J.	421	Wilson, D.
371	Bailey, A.C.	422	Yates, J.
372	Hayes, P.V.	423	Hill, W.
373	Twaits, C.H.	424	McCullum, A.

425	Knight, F.B.	476	Chilmaid, F.W.
426	Palliser, A.J.B.	477	Mouat, W.
427	Walker, S.	478	Farr, J.P.
428	Times, J.W.	479	Larter, A.C.
429	Cooper, V.A.	480	Harding, C.
430	Turner, R.N.	481	MacDonnell, E.R.
431	Crowe, J.T.	482	Defries, H.
432	Goodhue, F.W.J.	483	D'Oyley, R.
433	Boys, S.G.	484	Fulljames, T.
434	Mitchell, W.	485	Thomas, C.
435	Higgins, D.	486	Goodman, J.B.
436	Harris, F.	487	Jagger, J.J.
437	Rowley, H.B.	488	Walton, E.W.
438	Peters, W.A.	489	Clay, F.S.
439	Fraser, P. Neil.	490	Bradshaw, J.A.
440	Rigby, R.L.	491	King, P.E.
441	Stapleton, G.F.	492	Edwards, J.T.
442	Chivers, H.	493	Lewis, G.H.
443	Harrison, J.P.	494	Schofield, J.
444	Wraith, H.D.	495	Holiday, A.S.
445	Mallorie, T.P.	496	Bull, F.G.
446	Newman, T.B.	497	Ballard, J.J.
447	Crust, J.A.	498	Allan, J.T.
448	Clark, T.R.	499	Rowell, A.J.
449	Morrison, A.	500	Pollard, W.A.
450	Leach, A.	501	Whitelaw, W.H.
451	Burton, H.	502	Miller, J. McL.
452	Wylde, T.E.	503	Tringham, H.G.
453	Warter, H.D.W.T.	504	Hedger, C.A.
454	Woodward, H.W.	505	Stockting, C.
455	Hayne, R.	506	Clark, A.
456	Saxon, F.	507	Guntrip, F.A.W.
457	Broughton, J.	508	Sanderson, A.
458	Meadows, W.	509	Lillington, F.J.S.
459	Norwood, A.	510	Larking, A.G.

	Fraser, G.A.	511	Cullen, G.
461	Field, T.	512	Spurway, G.V.
462	Cadman, E.J.	513	Evans, G.L.B.
463	Goodall, A.H.	514	Pearson, F.J.
464	Beedle, W.H.	515	Featherstonehaugh, C.F.C.
465	Richardson, W.F.	516	Jones, A.A.
466	Murray, D.	517	Dixon-Spain, G.
467	Biggs, A.J.	518	Osborne, E.
468	Butler, B.D.	519	Collins, H.E.C.
469	Wellings, C.H.	520	Clemetson, D.L.
470	Harrison, A.E.	521	Wellings, G.B.
471	Baines, H.P.B.	522	Walker, S.
472	Walton, J.C.	523	Beeching, R.
473	Pippet, A.C.	524	Averill, H.C.
474	Birch, R.C.	525	Bruce, A.G.C.
475	Bentley, J.	526	Price, F.
527	Rushworth, J.A.	578	Godlonton, D.
528	Gandy, W.H.	579	Jackson, W.
529	Slaughter, A.E.	580	Hickling, H.
530	Clapham, J.P.	581	Batt, F.J.
531	Gason, R.	582	Kirby, L.
532	Webb, H.G.	583	Griffiths, J.W.
533	Lewis, M.	584	Taylor, W.
534	Rainbow, F.	585	Thomas, A.A.
535	Hilliar, E.J.M.	586	Pearson, J.
536	Fatt, C.F.	587	Walton, W.A.
537	Lewis, J.D.	588	Eynon, L.
538	Cooper, P.H.	589	Davies, W.
539	Broadribb, E.A.	590	Gregg, R.H.
540	Hertford, H.	591	Hemmant, J.W.
541	Haigh, J.J.	592	Tooze, H.J.M.
542	Pearce, R.	593	Robinson, A.
543	Leith, F.W.	594	Hodgkins, H.
544	Cooke, J.E.M.	595	Taylor, T.
545	Caulfield, G.B.	596	Butler, J.F.
546	Grant, J.L.G.	597	Bray, E.P.
547	Harvey, E.N.B.	598	Williams, F.T.
548	Perham, H.H.	599	Cheshire, J.H.C.
549	Mole, S.P.	600	Holder, H.J.
550	Morris, S.D.	601	Marchant, C.T.
551	Statham, B.C.J.H.	602	Pinkney, W.
552	Penfold, C.	603	Mundy, H.G.
553	Wood, C.	604	King-Webster, H.C.
554	Hammond, W.S.L.	605	Brown, O.S.
555	Barrington, G.	606	Bevan, T.
556	Evans, H.C.	607	Moore, C.A.
557	Pratt, E.E.	608	George, F.H.
558	Wyse, J.	609	Anderson, J.W.
559	Thompson, E.	610	Bland, E.L.
560	Davies, M.	611	Seabrook, W.G.
561	D'Aeth, E.H.H.	612	Healey, M.J.

	Hemingway, P.C.	613	Love, C.J.
563	Rivers, H.S.	614	Mackie, A.H.
564	Harding, J.T.	615	Turton, E.
565	Blake, L.L.	616	Hall, C.A.
566	Collier, F.	617	Rumley, G.H.
567	Wood, E.G.	618	Bandy, A.G.
568	Lawrence, W.F.	619	Catley, C.K.
569	White, W.H.	620	Bleuchamp, E.J.
570	Thomson, W.D.	621	Branson, C.F.
571	Atty, W.R.	622	Bolton, W.S.
572	Jones, D.G.J.	623	Butler, H.E.
573	Crippin, G.H.	624	Brown, F.H.
574	Goode, E. St. John.	625	Cunningham, T.L.
575	Gunning, H.M.	626	Berridge, J.
576	Cragg, E.	627	Connolly, J.A.
577	Balme, F.N.	628	Davies, B.E.
629	Oglethorpe, C.O.	680	Sennett, N.S.
630	Bishop, F.C.	681	Smith, J.M.
631	Chambers, H.M.	682	Sandland, G.
632	Hicks, A.C.D.	683	Gurney, T.H.
633	Canton, C.F.	684	Kirby, F.J.
634	Toogood, A.H.	685	Heffill, A.S.
635	Nicolaus, G.R.	686	Jacobs, I.
636	Clark, C.E.	687	Penfold, R.F.
637	Flynn, M.F.	688	Reynolds, A.
638	Tozer, A.E.	689	Worship, N.
639	James, F.	690	Dod, W.
640	Donoghue, O.	691	Reynolds, S.
641	Collin, L.F.	692	Lee, A.C.
642	Rodwell, A.E.T.	693	Plaistowe, E.
643	Cannon, F.	694	Ronaldson, C.R.
644	Marriott, R.B.	695	Brodrick, H.
645	Stacey, C.R.W.	696	Allen, H.E.
646	Bowles, W.A.	697	Pond, G.
647	Smiddy, J.G.	698	Barnes, L.H.
648	Barclay, J.L.	699	Woodthorpe, W.E.
649	Harvey, W.J.	700	Pine-Coffin, R.
650	Roach, L.V.	701	Miller, A.C.
651	Usborne, E.F.	702	Hopkins, H.
652	Ancell, M.	703	Hopkins, H.W.
653	Finucanne, P.	704	Humphreys, —
654	Smeaton, J.H.	705	Richards, H.J.
655	Wailes, J.M.	706	Bristow, S.R.
656	Munyard, F.W.	707	Lawton, J.W.S.
657	Fairweather, J.	708	Nutter, W.G.
658	Wrixon, R.M.	709	Tracy, P.J.
659	Maguire, C.	710	Nicholson, J.M.
660	Wrottesley, W.D.	711	Wright, Pte.
661	Knight, H.E.	712	Vyvyan, S.
662	Ward, F.W.	713	Berman, S.S.
663	Brambley, H.J.	714	Samson, A.W.

	Lownds, E.H.	715	Junkison, S.
665	Vickers, H.	716	Coyne, E.J.
666	Durham, J.M.B.	717	Rice, W.E.
667	Maulton, W.T.	718	Ryan, G.E.
668	Lake, F.S.	719	Ramsey, N.
669	Gedge, C.B.	720	Gottwaltz-Burkett, B.
670	Topham, J.W.	721	Summers, H.
671	Cox, F.H.	722	Rundall, W.H.
672	Hayward, C.B.	723	Reeves, D.H.
673	Firth, A.T.	724	Edwards, F.J.
674	William, R.W.	725	Seymour, T.
675	Hankin, G.H.	726	Ablett, E.V.W.
676	Parker, W.G.	727	Fletcher, J.
677	Battishill, J.H.	728	Evans, F.L.
678	Barlow, F.C.	729	Dell, J.
679	Colman, L.H.	730	Hill, H.W.
731	Diggs, W.L.C.	782	Jones, J.L.
732	West, T.J.	783	Thorne, C.
733	Meiggs, J.C.	784	Lewis, N.A.
734	Gibson, C.S.	785	Mercer, J.
735	Traynor, H.J.	786	Folliott, L.
736	Tolhurst, W.	787	Flemyng, M.C.
737	Linton, C.H.	788	Armstrong, W.B.
738	Stearns, H.	789	Jennings, T.
739	Topps, H.	790	Browning, P.R.
740	Smith, J.	791	Hurst, S.G.
741	Doyle, J.E.	792	Burt, T.M.
742	Stilwell, C.R.	793	Nowling, E.R.
743	Gladwin, T.	794	Mills, H.O.
744	Little, H.J.E.	795	Bullock, P.M.G.
745	Corbett, G.B.	796	Christophers, G.C.
746	Rowland, C.A.	797	Longman, P.B.
747	Stewart, C.	798	Shearn, F.W.
748	Fookes, A.C.	799	James, H.J.
749	Challenger, H.W.	800	Gracewood, G.M.
750	Webb, A.E.	801	Blaauw, H.T.G.
751	Westoby, C.F.	802	Tanner, F.W.
752	Bamkin, G.R.	803	Perry, F.
753	Hilson, A.E.	804	Davis, W.M.
754	Lynham, H.	805	Hodges, W.J.
755	Castle, G.P.	806	Ewing, G.
756	Ross, I.	807	Perry, O.
757	Way, H.A.L.	808	Wright, M.J.
758	Crundall, T.B.	809	Austin, L.
759	Eager, H.	810	Lomas, G.H.
760	Fenton, H.B.	811	Shepperson, B.E.
761	Taylor, E.F.H.	812	Burditt, H.
762	Ford, A.S.	813	Wilson, W.C.F.
763	Armstrong, S.	814	Hadley, E.J.
764	Reynolds, P.	815	Collen, R.
765	Dowker, F.H.	816	Tully, W.C.

	Donahoo, M.G.	817	Arnold, S.E.
767	Dewar, D.D.	818	Day, N.G.F.
768	Watson, J.L.	819	Jacobs, E.
769	Harrison, G.	820	Vernell, G.
770	Butler, H.J.	821	Clarke, L.
771	Paton, J.	822	Craven, J.
772	Everatt, W.T.	823	Winchcombe, F.
773	Madgwick, F.C.	824	Larner, D.H.
774	Beckingsale, B.L.	825	Wylie, J.H.
775	Hope, W.H.	826	Brown, R.
776	Miller, D.	827	Rushforth, E.G.
777	Humfrey, A.A.	828	Bowman, H.
778	Whalin, J.E.	829	James, M.E.C.
779	Carey, H.V.S.	830	Almond, G.
780	Faunch, T.S.	831	Bucknal, B.E.
781	Stockings, G.M.	832	Thompson, P.
833	Reynolds, T.	884	Blunden, F.
834	Brett, C.G.	885	Alexander, A.P.
835	Warner, D.R.	886	Powney, F.
836	Gaskell, C.E.	887	Mance, H.G.
837	Heal, W.G.	888	Mason, J.H.
838	Williams, R.S.	889	Weekes, M.G.
839	Dallow, C.B.	890	MacMahon, P.H.
840	West, W.C.	891	McRedmond, R.J.
841	Todd, P.G.	892	Cole, T.
842	Austin, R.E.	893	Winter, E.A.
843	Ward, J.S.	894	Bretherton, W.
844	Caris, S.	895	Dunn, A.E.
845	Lyons, J.L.	896	Tannett, G.
846	Gardner, A.F.	897	Hall, T.
847	Dale, R.P.	898	Balkwill, R.
848	Lane, R.	899	Gilmour, H.H.
849	Garnett, H.D.	900	Waterman, W.H.
850	Bufton, J.	901	Young, M.C.
851	Parkinson, J.	902	Whitlock, A.E.
852	Eccles, H.	903	Temple, H.
853	Brown, W.	904	Kemp, E.S.
854	Bates, G.	905	Vaughan-Williams, B.G.
855	Bennett, E.	906	Williams, M.L.
856	Diamond, J.A.	907	Simpson, A.
857	Welford, F.	908	Dean, J.G.
858	Shayler, J.H.	909	Doux, C.A. Le.
859	Davies, J.	910	Stobbs, S.
860	Waining, F.J.	911	Simms, J.
861	Doyle, J.J.	912	Kingsmill, G.
862	Roberts, J.	913	Fraser, L.
863	Duffy, T.	914	Turner, E.G.W.
864	Bee, J.	915	Johnson, C.A.
865	Seaman, W.D.	916	Roche, P.
866	Robins, I.J.	917	Cufie, W.
867	Burns, T.	918	Franklin, J.

Drew, C.
869 Race, S.
870 Young, J.W.L.
871 Cunneen, E.
872 Beverley, J.S.
873 McIntyre, A.
874 Mortimore, R.J.
875 Joyce, R.
876 Lloyd, H.T.
877 Webb, S.W.
878 Williams, C.
879 Tenniswood, J.
880 Buckley, T.S.
881 Watkins, H.
882 Merrick, J.J.
883 Stacpoole, R. de Vere.

919 Bates, W.E.
920 Backhouse, J.S.
921 Kendall, R.
922 Carter, R.J.
923 Noyes, R.T.
924 Knapp, F.G.
925 Dolby, G.E.
926 Christie, W.T.
927 Cox, A.
928 Muskin, J.
929 Smith, J.
930 Summers, J.C.
931 Wright, G.
932 Cairns, F.
933 Steward, J.S.
934 Pearce, H.E.R.

935 Kent, F.A.
936 Armstrong, C.
937 Kirton, W.
938 Clifford, S.
939 Holden, W.
940 Daniels, R.W.
941 Hartwell, G.A.
942 Bellamy, G.W.
943 Morrison, S.J.B.
944 Rutherford, W.A.
945 Michelsen, A.
946 Grove, E.A.
947 Hick, J.F.
948 Gibson, E.
949 Kennedy, A.J.
950 Walker, R.G.
951 Hartley, A.G.
952 Ross, G.S.
953 Gibb, R.A.
954 Sievier, E.H.P.
955 Baker, G.
956 Hillcoat, R.G.
957 Richard, W.C.
958 Brown, C.M.
959 Taylor, H.A.
960 Green, C.L.
961 Dowell, J.E.
962 Alexander, H.D.
963 Cairns, J.A.
964 Younger, F.N.
965 Cooke, S.M.
966 Shearm, A.
967 MacLennan, A.
968 Thorp, W.E.
969 MacKay, J.

986 Otter, W.H.
987 Marsh, A.J.
988 Hardy, E.A.
989 Newman, R.A.
990 Willcocks, N.
991 Bishop, S.M.
992 Graham, J.
993 Reddy, J.
994 Martin, J.G.
995 McGinness, J.
996 MacKay, D.
997 Inglis, D.S.
998 Macpherson, J.C.B.
999 Brett, W.H.
1000 Whitehead, W.
1001 Rowles, S.W.
1002 Cooper, W.F.
1003 Rosamond, A.
1004 Mudd, G.E.
1005 Dunn, E.H.
1006 Coleman, R.J.
1007 Broadribb, F.J.
1008 Priestley, A.G.B.
1009 Pipe, A.W.
1010 McCulloch, A.G.S.
1011 Campbell, P.
1012 Aikman, W.
1013 Smart, J.
1014 Borthwick, W.A.
1015 Willett, E.A.
1016 Fergusson, D.
1017 Morris, J.
1018 Watts, G.S.
1019 Alexander, A.
1020 Aitken, J.E.

	Challis, W.G.F.		
971	Hawley, D.	1021	Jones, C.C.
972	Thompson, J.	1022	Crookes, R.O.
973	Conolly, T.G.	1023	Stretton, W.J.
974	Hutchinson, D.F.	1024	Rhodes, M.L.
975	Dobinson, C.R.	1025	Skuse, L.N.
976	Myers, C.	1026	Scott, P.B.
977	Turnbull, J.A.	1027	Turner, D.P.
978	Mundell, W.	1028	Bourbel, D.A. de
979	Trusler, G.D.	1029	Dillon, C.
980	Woodard, A.M.W.	1030	Alexander, A.C.
981	McDonough, J.S.	1031	Foggo, W.D.
982	Kendall, R.	1032	Burnside, M.
983	Walker, D.F.	1033	Mather, W.M.
984	Stocken, T.H.L.	1034	Wilkinson, W.H.
985	Bagshaw, W.E.D.	1035	Richardson, G.
		1036	Kirby, W.J.A.

1037	Erskine, A.D.	1087	Gilmore, A.E.
1038	Anderson, J.J.	1088	Lelen, J.N.
1039	Brooks, F.	1089	Taylor, C.
1040	Ward, J.W.	1090	Hamilton, J.
1041	Jull, W.C.	1091	Greasley, G.
1042	Steggall, W.E.F.	1092	Hartley, C.W.
1043	Maughan, W.	1093	Fatt, C.H.
1044	Agnew, J.	1094	France, C.
1045	Black, W.	1095	Sinclair, F.K.
1046	Black, J.	1096	Dunn, H.
1047	Steele, J.	1097	Cochrane, W.E.
1048	Jones, W.E.G.	1098	Lethian, A.
1049	Hodgson, J.C.	1099	McWilliam, A.
1050	Stevenson, W.J.	1100	Rae, E.
1051	Muir, W.	1101	Black, W.
1052	Lees, W.A.C.	1102	Lauder, L.
1053	Burgess, C.W.	1103	Hockley, F.
1054	Greenstreet, T.W.	1104	Mansfield, E.
1055	Mason, S.H.	1105	Smith, W.
1056	Vickers, J.S.	1106	Hardaker, H.
1057	Ritchie, R.K.	1107	Sayer, L.C.
1058	Golding, E.	1108	Broomfield, J.C.
1059	Pitchford, E.E.	1109	Mark, W.
1060	Notley, F.	1110	Dunlop, C.
1061	James, B.E.	1111	Curwen, C.
1062	Boston, W.	1112	Jackson, S.
1063	Scovell, G.	1113	Gille, F.M.
1064	Parkins, H.	1114	Howarth, W.
1065	Dryburgh, J.	1115	Stark, J.
1066	Currie, W.	1116	Hamilton, J.
1067	Rattray, D.	1117	Hardie, A.
1068	Clunas, C.	1118	Moysen, G.
1069	Montgomerie-Fleming, J.B.	1119	Ballantine, A.
1070	Darrell, F.	1120	Wallace, D.H.
1071	Moir, A.W.	1121	Mackenzie, W.S.

	Cosnett, J.
1073	McKay, J.
1074	Kilpatrick, J.
1075	McRitchie, J.
1076	Paton, J.
1077	Henderson, D.
1078	Wainwright, H.L.
1079	Cochrane, J.
1080	Smith, A.H.
1081	Blumenthal, M.A.
1082	Stockbridge, J.M.
1083	Cumberland, W.J.
1084	Thomson, P.H.
1085	Hanbury, L.F.
1086	Parton, W.H.

1122	McFarquhar, M.
1123	Thomson, G.
1124	Anderson, A.
1125	O'Leary, C.E.
1126	Kinsley, L.M.
1127	Addis, A.J.
1128	Thompson, D.
1129	Thompson, S.
1130	MacKay, W.T.
1131	Fraser, A.C.
1132	Hayward, A.B.
1133	Smith, A.E.
1134	Smith, G.
1135	McClunie, T.
1136	Muirhead, J.
1137	Wilson, J.D.

1138	Geach, P.
1139	Walker, J.
1140	Kedey, A.H.
1141	Munro, A.
1142	Cockburn, J.
1143	Huggan, E.
1144	Smith, W.
1145	Denvers, R.N.
1146	Miller, R.S.
1147	Young, J.W.
1148	McMurtrie, J.H.T.
1149	Gough, A.
1150	Monteith, P.R.
1151	Anderson, J.C.M.
1152	McLaren, C.
1153	Bowes, W.
1154	Buchan, W.G.
1155	Cook, J.A.
1156	Ferguson, P.
1157	Johnstone, C.
1158	Seaton, W.M.
1159	Payne, R.H.
1160	Tyler, H.
1161	Whyte, F.J.
1162	Savile, H.M.
1163	Goodman, R.F.
1164	Wilson, W.
1165	Buchanan, J.M.L.
1166	Harding, H.G.
1167	Beadle, C.
1168	Waddington, T.T.
1169	Wale, A.
1170	Foran, W.R.
1171	Davies, H.
1172	Harling, E.

1189	Tremfield, A.
1190	Moffat, R.V.
1191	Scobell, W.B.
1192	Whiting, M.P.
1193	Chappell, J.C.
1194	Crafter, A.G.
1195	Denniford, P.W.
1196	Haybittel, L. McC.
1197	Gregor, A.
1198	Aspinwall, F.J.
1199	Mellett, I.E.
1200	Maclean, L.
1201	Munro, H.F.
1202	Eaton, H.
1203	Sampson, B.
1204	Webster, S.
1205	Cunnington, C.
1206	Oesterlein, F.S.
1207	Enderby, A.D.
1208	Baker, G.F.
1209	Gillam, G.
1210	Watkins, A.
1211	Lawrence, H.P.C.
1212	Philpot, H.
1213	Hendren, E.H.
1214	Jeffreys, C.W.
1215	Appleford, L.G.
1216	McCarnie, E.P.
1217	Goodman, S.T.
1218	Wheeler, F.G.
1219	Conquest, H.E.K.
1220	Smith, S.
1221	Brown, C.H.
1222	Simpson, W.
1223	Cleaver, T.J.

	Cooke, Sir W.H.		
1174	Lawson, F.B.	1224	Farrant, T.
1175	Marshall, C.C.	1225	MacNaughton, A.
1176	Logan, J.T.	1226	Bell, R.D.
1177	Tattam, J.	1227	James, E.A.
1178	Blake, P.V.	1228	Herd, C.
1179	Cook, J.	1229	Smith, H.E.
1180	Osborne, T.H.	1230	Steedman, R.S.
1181	Enderby, H.H.	1231	Reid, R.
1182	Cock, H.C.	1232	Kemp, J.D.
1183	Trickett, J.	1233	Ritchie, G.
1184	Hopkins, H.C.	1234	Thomson, W.
1185	Cross, E.J.	1235	Williams, P.A.
1186	De Vere West, H.	1236	Fenton, J.C.
1187	Weil, A.D.	1237	Reading, A.H.
1188	Gordon, H.S.	1238	Holley, H.C.
		1239	Pitts, E.
1240	Johnson, G.A.W.	1291	Owers, E.
1241	Williams, J.	1292	Callaghan, J.
1242	Stanley, R.	1293	Little, J.
1243	Trebilcock, J.R.	1294	McDiarmid, J.
1244	Goodfellow, H.	1295	Cairns, P.C.
1245	Fay, V.	1296	Thomas, T.W.
1246	Faulkner, A.	1297	Lovell, J.H.
1247	Buck, A.E.	1298	Steer, H.E.
1248	Littlewood, F.	1299	Haddon, J.
1249	Ashdown, W.C.	1300	McDonald, D.R.
1250	Vernon, J.P.	1301	Taylor, J.D.
1251	Anderson, S.D.	1302	Milleken, C.
1252	McCulloch, R.S.	1303	Remnant, P.W.
1253	Broadbridge, E.C.	1304	Saville, W.F.
1254	Garland, A.R.	1305	Vincer, E.S.
1255	Rogers, T.H.	1306	Davison, A.W.
1256	Scott-Tucker, H.B.H.	1307	Miller, C.J.
1257	Leith, E.	1308	Cassini, H.
1258	Petrie, F.	1309	Cross, W.
1259	Dalton, J.S.M.	1310	Hutchins, G.
1260	Mowat, W.G.	1311	Chinnock, C.
1261	Barker-Mill, T.R.S.V.	1312	Adams, F.
1262	Munro, A.W.	1313	Parkinson, H.F.
1263	McPhee, J.A.	1314	Nunn, H.E.
1264	Heron, J.	1315	Osgood, F.
1265	Scott, G.G.	1316	Harris, J.F.
1266	Deakin, C.	1317	Cameron, A.S.
1267	Hughes, W.l.	1318	Cran, C.F.
1268	Gowton, C.	1319	Allan, W.
1269	Bennett, G.	1320	Lindsay, E.
1270	Sullivan, D.H.	1321	Strachan, J.
1271	Lawrence, B.E.	1322	Fletcher, J.F.
1272	Attwood, C.	1323	Cooper, S.A.A.
1273	Buckland, H.F.	1324	Jones, B.
1274	Gibson, G.R.	1325	Kirk, H.

	Hannah, R.	1326	Mansfield, G.A.
1276	Galloway, S.	1327	Legg, H.
1277	McFarlane, J.	1328	Jones, W.H.
1278	Bryden, T.	1329	Field, R.J.H.
1279	Grant, D.	1330	Sylvester, J.W.
1280	Johnstone, W.	1331	Wickens, E.J.
1281	Laycock, P.G.O.	1332	Rogers, W.H.
1282	Laycock, R.A.	1333	Wilson, J.
1283	Wedemeyer, P.E.	1334	Green, G.H.
1284	Stewart, P.C.	1335	Slaughter, M.F.
1285	Ferris, R.	1336	McGeoch, J.
1256	Lemen, R.	1337	Johnstone, C.
1287	Walker, J.V.	1338	Kidd, G.
1288	Williamson, J.	1339	Robertson, D.F.
1289	Gilmour, J.M.	1340	Sutherland, W.
1290	Morgan, R.	1341	Johnson, J.A.
1342	Bray, P.B.R.	1393	Northcote, S.W.
1343	De Lara, G.	1394	Kearns, S.C.
1344	Foreman, W.A.	1395	Gwatkin, T.
1345	Suttie, W.F.	1396	Goad, H.
1346	McCormach, W.J.	1397	Scott, W.J.
1347	Gowton, T.W.	1398	Steggall, R.F.
1348	Wake, J.	1399	Ward, G.
1349	Travis, J.	1400	Goomer, W.
1350	Macpherson, W.	1401	Wilkinson, J.T.
1351	Anderson, T.A.	1402	Davies, P.R.M.
1352	Lovering, W.R.	1403	Smeaton, H.
1353	Crawford, H.A.	1404	Field, E.
1354	Clarke, E.A.	1405	Donn, R.
1355	Hollingsworth, E.	1406	Robertson, D.L.
1356	Kingston, N.L.I.	1407	Gurteen, S.
1357	McDonald, J.D.	1408	Galbraith, C.A.
1358	Carmichael, D.C.	1409	Seton, S.
1359	Luke, A.T.	1410	Taylor, J.
1360	Sullivan, R.H.	1411	Hudson, W.
1361	West, E.J.	1412	Wilkinson, W.C.
1362	Whelband, E.	1413	Cooke, E.G.
1363	Pimm, E.J.	1414	Powell, W.F.
1364	James, R.	1415	Brown, J.
1365	Drury, J.J.R.	1416	Moir, A.E.
1366	Robertson, W.	1417	Hart, S.
1367	Mackrory, E.W.	1418	Crabb, R.
1368	Martin, G.	1419	Robbie, J.
1369	Carswell, D.	1420	McNab, W.
1370	Dunbar, W.P.	1421	McGregor, H.
1371	Lindsay, R.	1422	Foster, H.
1372	Rosie, P.	1423	Seath, D.
1373	Donald, G.R.	1424	Dodds, W.J.
1374	Dunbar, T.M.	1425	Lee, W.J.
1375	Beaven, F.L.	1426	Banks, J.H.
1376	Spencer, A.	1427	Walker, V.D.

	Broadley, C.	1428	Naylor, H.S.
1378	Monour, J.	1429	Watson, J.
1379	Chambers, T.	1430	Coyle, J.
1380	Bell, R.	1431	Delaney, J.
1381	White, C.	1432	Forster, F.L.M.
1382	Gibson, J.M.	1433	Smith, W.H.
1383	Thomson, F.	1434	Batson, G.
1384	Neal, S.E.	1435	Martin, W.J.
1385	Baker, L.F.	1436	Wisdom, R.
1386	Niblett, W.F.	1437	Hopley, C.F.C.
1387	Cummings, G.A.	1438	Guy, A.
1388	Clark, N.	1439	Bardell, W.E.
1389	Gotthardt, C.F.	1440	Nicoll, J.H.
1390	Robertson, J.	1441	Fraser, A.
1391	Fraser, M.	1442	Packer, J.T.
1392	McKay, A.	1443	Barnes, H.

1444	Grocott, G.N.G.	1495	Anderson, D.
1445	Hopegood, F.L. Vere.	1496	Wild, A.H.
1446	Bullock, E.	1497	Rogers, R.M.
1447	Hummerston, W.J.	1498	Beath, H.W.
1448	Whiteside, H.	1499	Ewing, A.D.
1449	Page, W.	1500	Lawes, F.H.
1450	Hogan, P.L.	1501	England, R.
1451	Eley, C.W.	1502	Larkin, H.G.L.
1452	Orme, J.	1503	Buckton, A.W.
1453	Bingham, C.	1504	Bell, J.S.
1454	Dean, F.N.	1505	Guest, E.F.
1455	Marnie, A.S.	1506	Clark, W.W.
1456	Luke, W.T.	1507	Marshall, H.C.
1457	Brown, H.C.	1508	Clarke, A.H.
1458	Purgavie, F.	1509	Simpson, J.
1459	Purgavie, W.R.	1510	Taunt-Ward, G.
1460	Love, J.R.	1511	Rudd, H.B.
1461	Senior, F.	1512	Cameron, J.J.
1462	Crowley, E.T.	1513	Brown, J.
1463	Sutherland, A.	1514	Ion, W.
1464	Lort, W.V.	1515	Watson, J.W.
1465	Taylor, J.H.	1516	Price, H.O.
1466	Phillips, O.F.	1517	Maddern, W.H.T.
1467	Harrison, J.	1518	Nelson, W.
1468	McCarroll, J.	1519	Downham, E.J.
1469	Albany, G.A.	1520	Jones, T.W.
1470	Keillor, W.	1521	Robinson, J.W.
1471	Robertson, D.M.	1522	Smith, W.
1472	Brown, R.L.	1523	Drake, J.W.
1473	Clarke, C.	1524	Hodge, R.N.
1474	Coats, A.C.	1525	Hodges, W.S.
1475	Vickery, G.H.	1526	Walsh, W.M.
1476	Lord, G.H.	1527	Seale, G.D.
1477	Kington, M.W.	1528	Nops, R.A.
1478	Wilson, A.V.	1529	Cook, J.

	Parr, H.E.	1530	Gemmell, G.M.
1480	Farmer, W.	1531	Le Butt, C.W.N.
1481	Randall, W.	1532	Ward, A.
1482	Gay, W.	1533	Walter, J.H.
1483	Carnochan, J.	1534	Fryett, F.
1484	McFarlane, J.	1535	Wilson, R.
1485	Bond, B.	1536	Doig, W.
1486	Vines, J.	1537	Goldspink, L.
1487	Phillips, J.H.	1538	Pratt, H.W.
1488	Riddell, M.	1539	Buptie, J.W.
1489	Arnot, J.S.	1540	Sheridan, J.W.
1490	Green, H.	1541	Smith, R.B.
1491	Townshend, C.	1542	Took, E.A.
1492	Bradley, H.L.	1543	Jones, T.C.L.
1493	Follett, G.	1544	Lovibond, R.F.
1494	Crombie, H.	1545	Cogswell, A.
1546	Moss, J.	1597	Harbott, W.G.
1547	Cannon, E.	1598	Bradford, S.
1548	Cheesman, S.F.	1599	Harrington, A.
1549	Morris, G.	1600	Fitzgerald, F.
1550	Howe, J.D.	1601	Cooper, W.H.
1551	Strachan, J.	1602	Lefever, J.F.
1552	Cook, J.K.	1603	Kildare, T.J.
1553	McDougall, J.	1604	Browning, E.
1554	Scherer, C.	1605	Howell, W.R.
1555	King, D.	1606	Maxwell, A.R.
1556	Misset, M.	1607	Pinson, I.L.
1557	Watt, R.S.	1608	Bradberry, T.R.
1558	Hurst, C.	1609	Rubidge, H.W.
1559	Hurlbatt, E.	1610	Barnes, S.
1560	Kloss, A.	1611	White, L.T.
1561	Dowdswell, H.	1612	Simpson, A.B.
1562	Duncan, W.	1613	Argles, G.E.
1563	Smith, R.	1614	Arbone, L.G.
1564	Jones, R.	1615	Calderwood, A.
1565	Boycott, F.E.	1616	Leigh, F.A.
1566	Miles, P.A.	1617	Lamb, A.G.
1567	Miles, A.	1618	Stafford, W.D.
1568	Lawrence, C.E.	1619	Wilson, J.J.
1569	Banks, C.T.	1620	Edwards, C.W.
1570	Bennett, W.	1621	Walker, G.W.
1571	Penson, W.S.	1622	Over, C.A.
1572	Levy, H.P.	1623	Taylor, O.G.
1573	Cox, F.	1624	Baker, J.
1574	Hardcastle, J.W.	1625	Dean, F.
1575	Pearce, F.	1626	Crone, W.C.
1576	Smith, A.W.	1627	George, T.E.
1577	Stewart, T.A.	1628	Wilkey, F.D.
1578	Barnett, F.T.	1629	Kennelly, R.V.V.
1579	Pettit, W.	1630	Whitehurst, A.
1580	Arnott, D.	1631	Black, R.W.

	Wright, C.	1632	Scott, W.B.
1582	Wright, S.C.H.	1633	Middleton, T.S.
1583	Tracy, G.	1634	Willcocks, J.C.
1584	Beckett, G.A.	1635	Scott, E.
1585	Barrett, T.	1636	Freeman, E.P.
1586	Edwards, E.	1637	Hanwell, A.
1587	Ambler, R.	1638	Prince, A.T.
1588	Bowen, H.C.	1639	Whyte, W.E.
1589	Beaver, W.J.	1640	Dobb, H.S.
1590	Ogle, A.H.	1641	Manardo, T.S.
1591	Loveland, H.	1642	Wright, G.M.D.
1592	Rider, W.	1643	Cripps, F.
1593	Gardner, A.	1644	Merwood, J.W.
1594	Cottrell, H.J.	1645	Newman, R.G.
1595	Harvey, J.J.	1646	Harding, J.
1596	Stirrups, A.T.	1647	Littman, S.
1648	McGibson, J.	1699	Grandin, J.W.
1649	Saywood, G.	1700	Moulding, W.
1650	Martin, H.G.	1701	Curryer, R.W.
1651	Fine, A.L.	1702	Wilkin, W.
1652	Gaul, E.	1703	Allen, A.
1653	Bradford, W.H.	1704	Smith, A.
1654	Coupland, J.	1705	Jeffery, A.E.
1655	Johnston, G.G.	1706	Grout, H.
1656	Rait, D.	1707	Gilbert, C.F.
1657	Bell, T.S.	1708	Pepper, C.
1658	Gensey, C.	1709	Wakefield, T.
1659	Cummins, G.	1710	Brown, G.
1660	Clark, J.	1711	Cook, S.
1661	Manning, E.	1712	Anderson, A.J.
1662	Holmes, W.J.	1713	Ferrier, J.K.
1663	Timms, D.G.	1714	Atkins, S.A.V.
1664	Ellis, R.	1715	Sorley, J.
1665	Wheatley, C.C.	1716	Read, E.S.
1666	Thorning, S.	1717	Skinner, C.W.H.
1667	Gilder, R.A.	1718	Paddon, G.W.
1668	Herring, R.	1719	Rutherford, P.J.
1669	Sutton, H.	1720	Smith, R.
1670	Biggs, C.P.	1721	Raymond, F.
1671	Slipper, R.S.	1722	Harding, S.
1672	Fryett, A.M.	1723	Elliott, B.D.
1673	Fraser, E.	1724	Watkin, F.A.
1674	Walford, F.G.	1725	Owen, H.
1675	McFarlane, H.	1726	Walton, J.M.
1676	Saunders, S.	1727	Collier, G.E.
1677	Wright, H.	1728	Cann, H.E.
1678	Brown, R.S.	1729	Bartlett, E.
1679	Lee, C.	1730	Rayner, C.
1680	Procter, G.J.	1731	Monkman, F.K.
1681	Crane, J.	1732	Aldred, H.D.
1682	Galbraith, A.	1733	Hyde, A.W.

	Simons, L.		
1684	Ling, H.	1734	Harrison, E.F.
1685	Kimpton, J.	1735	Johnston, J.H.
1686	Joyner, G.R.	1736	Calder, J.H.
1687	Lowther, W.	1737	Mock, K.A.D.
1688	Jones, W.D.P.	1738	Bristow, R.J.S.
1689	Rogers, J.F.W.	1739	Brown, A.E.
1690	Lewis, A.	1740	Harrison, H.J.
1691	Hodge, A.	1741	Hickson, W.G.
1692	Anderson, W.	1742	Read, J.
1693	Gillett, W.R.F.	1743	Tomalin, R.A.
1694	Partridge, E.	1744	Podger, A.H.
1695	Cutler, W.E.	1745	Fletcher, S.A.
1696	Keeble, G.H.	1746	Rogers, B.F.
1697	Cant, W.H.	1747	Edwards, H.J.
1698	Fox, C.F.	1748	Jewell, C.R.
		1749	Denyer, F.H.

1750	Bell, J.W.	1801	Davies, C.A.
1751	Bullard, A.R.	1802	Wilson, G.
1752	Deller, S.G.	1803	Dodman, A.S.
1753	Bell, W.L.	1804	Warman, W.C.
1754	Mostyn, F.	1805	Luxton, W.
1755	Lemon, F.G.	1806	Brown, H.G.
1756	Smith, H.E.S.	1807	Burchett, J.G.
1757	Hall, A.M.	1808	Horsley, W.E.
1758	Ashwood, W.	1809	Brown, A.O.
1759	Baldock, W.P.	1810	Snodgrass, A.E.
1760	Croxford, H.J.	1811	Baker, F.
1761	Ford, F.H.	1812	Dodman, C.A.
1762	Fright, E.G.	1813	Taylor, F.
1763	Pay, S.	1814	Macfarlane, A.
1764	Sharp, W.H.	1815	Neil, D.A.
1765	Weal, C.A.	1816	Beavan, J.R.
1766	Palmer, H.C.	1817	Paget, F.F.
1767	Dunne, J.	1818	Jewell, J.O.
1768	Cox, E.C.	1819	Conquest, E.J.
1769	Titley, E.J.	1820	Garnish, G.A.
1770	Sandland, C.K.	1821	Curtis, A.E.J.
1771	Williams, R.G.	1822	Hyde, A.G.
1772	Charlier, H.H.	1823	Webber, T.E.
1773	Ramsay, F.G.	1824	Ingham, H.G.
1774	Anderson, J.G.	1825	Crisp, H.J.
1775	Gore, J.T.	1826	Middleton, W.E.C.
1776	Morris, A.W.T.	1827	Mackenzie, W.
1777	Taylor, A.W.	1828	Call, W.S.
1778	Hunter, H.P.	1829	Wilkinson, H.
1779	Briden, A.C.	1830	Holmes, J.B.F.
1780	Tapping, C.F.	1831	Fletcher, S.P.
1781	Leppard, S.	1832	Brook, T.
1782	Tandy, S.T.	1833	Abbott, G.H.
1783	Cotgrove, E.G.	1834	Fowles, J.P.A.
1784	Scott, F.S.	1835	Connolly, M.

	Ditchfield, H.		
1786	Taylor, M.	1836	Pollard, H.J.
1787	McKercher, C.	1837	Knight, L.D.
1788	Read, J.	1838	Pollard, G.E.
1789	Wollnough, H.W.	1839	Sheppard, W.S.
1790	Fox, J.W.	1840	Sheppard, W.J.
1791	Cooper, G.T.	1841	Heaver, P.G.
1792	Jennings, R.S.	1842	Walker, E.
1793	Martin, E.	1843	Rollason, W.A.
1794	Clarke, R.J.	1844	McCarthy, W.E.
1795	Wilks, E.L.	1845	Fisher, J.H.K.
1796	Murray, C.F.	1846	Cripps, R.
1797	Stokes, A.E.	1847	Brewer, A.H.
1798	Stokes, J.E.	1848	Cromarty, R.R.
1799	Barham, T.G.	1849	Meldrum, A.J.
1800	Bown, H.E.	1850	Fox, J.F.
		1851	Thomas, R.G.

1852	Simpson, W.	1903	Smith, F.C.
1853	Fayrer, H.W.J.	1904	Taylor, C.W.
1854	Fleming, S.J.	1905	Taylor, L.H.
1855	Bibby, J.	1906	Pike, W.T.
1856	Drage, E.G.	1907	Ford, H.F.
1857	French, G.A.	1908	Robins, E.G.
1858	Brett, S.A.	1909	Hawkesworth, K.
1859	Haggis, S.G.	1910	Webb, J.W.
1860	Hayes, L.H.	1911	Sheppard, J.
1861	Davies, A.E.	1912	Phipps, E.G.
1862	Nancarrow, C.W.	1913	Martin, E.W.
1863	Jenkin, W.	1914	Barnes, F.
1864	Pellymounter, W.J.	1915	Young, W.J.
1865	Prizeman, N.	1916	Vanstone, H.A.
1866	Pearcey, J.C.	1917	Hampson, H.
1867	Sim, V.D.	1918	Hatchard, H.
1868	Burrow, R.J.	1919	Hunt, W.
1869	Mayne, H.R.	1920	Durrant, F.J.
1870	Blount, J.G.	1921	Brayley, C.
1871	Bennett, F.J.	1922	Robertson, J.H.
1872	Miller, F.N.	1923	Watson, C.H.
1873	Older, H.E.	1924	Niblett, H.
1874	Hamley, W.	1925	Harden, C.A.
1875	Haywood, J.	1926	Saltern, G.H.
1876	Hansell, S.G.	1927	Barton, L.B.
1877	Wekks, T.A.	1928	Monk, A.C.
1878	McPhail, P.	1929	Naylor, J.M.
1879	Sampson, T.R.	1930	Marshall, A.F.
1880	Fawns, J.M.	1931	Billett, T.W.
1881	Boyce, F.J.	1932	Fulcher, S.
1882	Summers, G.W.	1933	McFarlane, T.
1883	Dielham, S.C.	1934	Watt, W.J.C.
1884	Coyle, F.J.	1935	Bangs, P.R.
1885	Stinson, T.H.	1936	Ryan, W.A.W.
1886	Wood, W.F.	1937	Kay, H.G.

	Newcombe, H.W.	1938	Penchoen, E.T.
1888	Gunston, W.	1939	Watson, T.M.
1889	Malcholm, P.R.	1940	King, W.
1890	Broadbridge, S.H.R.	1941	Hartgrove, E.W.
1891	Woodward, G.T.	1942	Cable, M.
1892	Tapp, J.H.	1943	Freshwater, H.
1893	Blofield, —	1944	Stains, J.J.
1894	Wilkins, H.	1945	Frith, H.G.
1895	Cornish, A.	1946	Carter, E.A.
1896	Read, F.C.	1947	Squeaker, G. Pritchard.
1897	Hathaway, A.	1948	Vokes, E.
1898	Grant, S.W.	1949	Dickeson, W.G.
1899	Mitchell, A.L.	1950	Hurst, J.
1900	Rundle, H.W.	1951	Titchener, A.
1901	White, F.C.	1952	Wilson, W.
1902	North, C.G.	1953	Kavanagh, J.E.P.
1954	Glanvil, P.C.	3414	Ward, H.W.
1955	Grover, V.E.	3427	Williams, C.H.
1956	Smith, H.B.S.	2768	Yates, R.
1957	Curtis, A.C.	5915	Wheeler, —
1958	Sporne, A.R.	10810	Jones, E.T.
1959	Briggs, H.A.	3840	Prior, H.L.
1960	Whitelaw, D.	3888	Bibby, C.
1961	Parker, A.H.	3913	Colton, R.
1962	Howett, F.	3801	Hichie, G.
1963	Piper, C.	3885	Mason, E.W.
1964	Cartlidge, J.A.	2063	Ball, C.S.
1965	Dykes, G.F.	3820	Whipps, J.
1966	Nettleton, A.	4076	Adamson, J.
1967	King, G.W.	3937	Sothcott, J.G.
1968	Dunn, F.W.	3520	Moss, F.A.
1969	James, S.	3853	Pearce, W.
1970	Collings, W.	3827	Reeman, A.W.
1971	Denyer, A.E.	2735	Tremayne, D.
1972	Bartram, F.A.	3855	Hart, F.G.T.
1973	Deares, H.	3836	Colbert, H.S.
1974	Browning, A.E.	3856	Crafter, D.T.
1975	Hooker, G.H.	3812	Dilloway, W.
1976	Eastland, F.C.	3857	Gretton, L.
1977	Reynolds, R.	3926	Rose, J.T.
1978	Heathcote, J.	3904	Shawcroft, F.
1979	Dunn, E.E.	3809	Hichie, G.D.C.
1980	English, E.W.	3922	Willes, A.
1981	Smith, J.F.	3892	Allenby, T.
1982	Fogerty, J.H.A.	3894	Lindow, H.
1983	Bennett, N.C.	3910	McCarthy, J.
1984	Meade, M.	3905	Ottewell, J.W.
1965	Robbins, A.	3902	Parkin, W.
1986	St. John, W.P.	3903	Steed, S.
1987	Arnold, G.	3819	Turner, F.
1988	Clitter, E.W.	3011	Arthur, H.E.

	Chinn, F.H.	3880	Bailey, H.
1990	Hart, C.J.	3794	Baker, W.G.
1991	Prime, S.M.	3225	Barker, A.R.
1992	Richards, E.W.	3817	Beck, S.
1993	Buccleuch, C.	2962	Bridgman, A.F.
1994	George, G.W.	3843	Degerton, A.N.
1995	Maxwell, R.G.	3253	Distin, T.
1996	Cottee, H.E.	3933	Dobran, T.H.
1997	Baker, W.	3492	Fowler, F.G.
1998	Crawford, J.E.	3433	Fowler, H.W.
1999	Oaksford, H.	3555	Thomas, J.F.
2000	Harwood, G.	3559	Law, M.C.
2765	Kerr, W.H.	3560	Simpson, C.
3318	Mitchell, T.P.	3568	Perren, F.
3156	Mitton, R.W.	3585	Ralph, F.C.
3528	Moss, F.A.	3592	Kirk, H.
3145	Walkerley, F.J.	3605	Stares, J.
3623	Lloyd, A.	4001	Mellor, J.
3627	Gillham, A.	4002	Alexander, T.
3729	Schobius, A.G.	4003	Kitchener, A.J.
3630	McCarthy, D.	4004	Osborne, J.T.
3631	Buxton, J.	4005	Long, H.S.
3635	Parsons, J.L.	4006	Robinson, T.H.
3640	Clark-Schroder, S.J.	4007	Benedict, F.W.
3643	Freeborn, B.	4008	Mogford, A.C.
3657	Hart, R.O.	4009	Underwood, H.
3660	Spencer, A.	4010	Wood, L.
3667	Epstein, B.S.	4011	Miles, F.J.
3673	Butler, C.	4012	Edwards, E.B.
3683	Woodward, E.	4013	Foan, W.D.
3684	Ulph, W.P.	4014	Dingley, A.W.
3690	Page, G.W.	4015	Monk, E.W.
3695	Towler, H.	4016	Warrell, F.C.
3702	Redwood, W.	4017	Miller, A.
3720	Smith, S.	4018	Coutts-Hill, W.H.
3737	Chetminoki, H.	4019	Benvie, A.S.
3738	McGowan, F.S.	4020	White, A.J.
3740	McDonald, A.A.	4021	Wood, W.G.
3742	Jolly, A.R.	4022	Hackett, F.T.
3750	Brodie, C.F.	4023	Hyslop, —
3780	Glasgow, M.R.	4024	Beach, W.J.
3787	Banfield, A.F.	4025	Howden, J.
3822	Gabbey, W.J.	4026	Sellers, C.
3829	Cheers, D.H.	4027	Hannay, A.
3830	Cornes, H.	4028	Gibbs, G.J.
3842	Barrass, G.S.	4029	Balls, E.
3851	Ayland, R.P.	4030	Ransley, W.J.
3886	Collins, M.	4031	Tomlinson, R.F.
3895	Grape, H.S.	4032	Simmons, R.W.
3911	Piper, W.H.	4033	Leat, F.C.
3930	Dutton, G.F.	4034	Elley, C.H.

	Bardell, R.J.		
3213	Ahronsberg, S.	4035	Ashby, E.A.
3546	Baptist, H.B.J.	4041	Beech, T.
3462	Barnbrook, A.E.	4042	Sniders, A.
2962	Bridgman, F.	4043	Budd, B.
3474	Brook, H.	4044	Mills, A.E.
2329	Cocks, E.M.	4046	Caskie, F.J.
3190	German, W.H.	4051	Doe, H.
3085	Hogg, D.A.	4053	Smith, H.R.
3394	Gilbert, F.G.	4056	Wain, G.H.
3859	Godfree, C.S.	4057	Stevens, W.H.
3844	Morris, F.	4060	Cocks, J.E.
3906	Parr, C.	4061	Hoile, D.H.
3907	Parr, E.A.	4063	Bevan, H.C.
2886	Price, W.J.A.	4068	Cargill, W.R.
3826	Randell, P.G.	4070	Gilkerson, J.C.
3862	Vernall, F.A.	4073	Lewis, F.
3250	Young, F.E.	4074	Chambers, R.S.
		4075	James, H.

ALSO FROM LEONAUR

OMPTEDA OF THE KING'S GERMAN LEGION *by Christian von Ompteda*—A Hanoverian Officer on Campaign Against Napoleon.

LIEUTENANT SIMMONS OF THE 95TH (RIFLES) *by George Simmons*—Recollections of the Peninsula, South of France & Waterloo Campaigns of the Napoleonic Wars.

A HORSEMAN FOR THE EMPEROR *by Jean Baptiste Gazzola*—A Cavalryman of Napoleon's Army on Campaign Throughout the Napoleonic Wars.

SERGEANT LAWRENCE *by William Lawrence*—With the 40th Regt. of Foot in South America, the Peninsular War & at Waterloo.

CAMPAIGNS WITH THE FIELD TRAIN *by Richard D. Henegan*—Experiences of a British Officer During the Peninsula and Waterloo Campaigns of the Napoleonic Wars.

CAVALRY SURGEON *by S. D. Broughton*—On Campaign Against Napoleon in the Peninsula & South of France During the Napoleonic Wars 1812-1814.

MEN OF THE RIFLES *by Thomas Knight, Henry Curling & Jonathan Leach*—The Reminiscences of Thomas Knight of the 95th (Rifles) by Thomas Knight, Henry Curling's Anecdotes by Henry Curling & The Field Services of the Rifle Brigade from its Formation to Waterloo by Jonathan Leach.

THE ULM CAMPAIGN 1805 *by F. N. Maude*—Napoleon and the Defeat of the Austrian Army During the 'War of the Third Coalition'.

SOLDIERING WITH THE 'DIVISION' *by Thomas Garrety*—The Military Experiences of an Infantryman of the 43rd Regiment During the Napoleonic Wars.

SERGEANT MORRIS OF THE 73RD FOOT *by Thomas Morris*—The Experiences of a British Infantryman During the Napoleonic Wars-Including Campaigns in Germany and at Waterloo.

A VOICE FROM WATERLOO *by Edward Cotton*—The Personal Experiences of a British Cavalryman Who Became a Battlefield Guide and Authority on the Campaign of 1815.

NAPOLEON AND HIS MARSHALS *by J. T. Headley*—The Men of the First Empire.

LEONAUR

ALSO FROM LEONAUR
AVAILABLE IN SOFTCOVER OR HARDCOVER WITH DUST JACKET

CAPTAIN COIGNET *by Jean-Roch Coignet*—A Soldier of Napoleon's Imperial Guard from the Italian Campaign to Russia and Waterloo.

HUSSAR ROCCA *by Albert Jean Michel de Rocca*—A French cavalry officer's experiences of the Napoleonic Wars and his views on the Peninsular Campaigns against the Spanish, British And Guerilla Armies.

MARINES TO 95TH (RIFLES) *by Thomas Fernyhough*—The military experiences of Robert Fernyhough during the Napoleonic Wars.

LIGHT BOB *by Robert Blakeney*—The experiences of a young officer in H.M 28th & 36th regiments of the British Infantry during the Peninsular Campaign of the Napoleonic Wars 1804 - 1814.

WITH WELLINGTON'S LIGHT CAVALRY *by William Tomkinson*—The Experiences of an officer of the 16th Light Dragoons in the Peninsular and Waterloo campaigns of the Napoleonic Wars.

SERGEANT BOURGOGNE *by Adrien Bourgogne*—With Napoleon's Imperial Guard in the Russian Campaign and on the Retreat from Moscow 1812 - 13.

SURTEES OF THE 95TH (RIFLES) *by William Surtees*—A Soldier of the 95th (Rifles) in the Peninsular campaign of the Napoleonic Wars.

SWORDS OF HONOUR *by Henry Newbolt & Stanley L. Wood*—The Careers of Six Outstanding Officers from the Napoleonic Wars, the Wars for India and the American Civil War.

ENSIGN BELL IN THE PENINSULAR WAR *by George Bell*—The Experiences of a young British Soldier of the 34th Regiment 'The Cumberland Gentlemen' in the Napoleonic wars.

HUSSAR IN WINTER *by Alexander Gordon*—A British Cavalry Officer during the retreat to Corunna in the Peninsular campaign of the Napoleonic Wars.

THE COMPLEAT RIFLEMAN HARRIS *by Benjamin Harris as told to and transcribed by Captain Henry Curling, 52nd Regt. of Foot*—The adventures of a soldier of the 95th (Rifles) during the Peninsular Campaign of the Napoleonic Wars.

THE ADVENTURES OF A LIGHT DRAGOON *by George Farmer & G.R. Gleig*—A cavalryman during the Peninsular & Waterloo Campaigns, in captivity & at the siege of Bhurtpore, India.

www.ingramcontent.com/pod-product-compliance
Lightning Source LLC
Chambersburg PA
CBHW031902090426
42741CB00005B/602